SELECTED
POEMS
OF
ANNE
SEXTON

Books by Anne Sexton

POETRY

To Bedlam and Part Way Back / 1960
All My Pretty Ones / 1962
Live or Die / 1966
Love Poems / 1969
Transformations / 1971
The Book of Folly / 1972
The Death Notebooks / 1974
The Awful Rowing Toward God / 1975
45 Mercy Street / 1976
Words for Dr. Y.: Uncollected Poems / 1978
The Complete Poems / 1981

PROSE

Anne Sexton: A Self-Portrait in Letters / 1977

SELECTED POEMS OF ANNE SEXTON

EDITED WITH
AN INTRODUCTION BY

Diane Wood Middlebrook
AND Diana Hume George

Houghton Mifflin Company

Boston ❦ 1988

Copyright © 1988 by Linda Gray Sexton, as Literary Executor
of the Estate of Anne Sexton.
Introduction © 1988 by Diane Wood Middlebrook and Diana Hume George.
All rights reserved.

For information about permission to reproduce selections from this book,
write to Permissions, Houghton Mifflin Company, 2 Park Street,
Boston, Massachusetts 02108.

Library of Congress Cataloging-in-Publication Data

Sexton, Anne.
Selected poems of Anne Sexton.

I. Middlebrook, Diane Wood. II. George, Diana Hume,
date.   III. Title.
PS3537.E915 A6   1988   811'.54   87-34253
ISBN 0-395-44595-7
ISBN 0-395-47782-4 (pbk.)

Printed in the United States of America

P 10 9 8 7 6 5 4 3 2 1

Contents

v

From All My Pretty Ones (1962)

From Live or Die (1966)

From The Awful Rowing Toward God (1975)

Posthumously Published Work

Words for Dr. Y. (1978)

From Letters to Dr. Y.

From Scorpio, Bad Spider, Die: The Horoscope Poems

From Last Poems

Introduction

Anne Sexton is that rare creature in American culture, a popular poet. Her career coincided with an era in American history — the 1960s and the early 1970s — when audiences for poetry sought relevance and immediacy and liked to watch poets perform in public. Sexton's work appealed to such audiences. Simple, forceful imagery made her work accessible, and she wrote about subjects that attracted interest: mental breakdown, sex, addiction, abortion — the other side of ordinary life in the suburbs. But stepping to the podium in the long dresses she wore for public readings, Anne Sexton seemed anything but ordinary. Kicking off her shoes, lighting a cigarette, she would read, in her marvelous, throaty, classy voice, harrowing accounts of insanity and loss. She was an artist; her purpose was to make awesome experiences lively, immediate, and real.

Though onstage Sexton was an exciting, glamorous reader, she suffered periods of suicidal self-hatred for which she was hospitalized in mental institutions and treated with psychoactive drugs. Sexton often claimed that poetry kept her alive; writing gave her a way to work out an understanding of herself *and* the culture that underlay her multiple pathologies. Many people in her large audiences seized on her words as revealing a condition they shared. She was very much a poet of her time.

Most of Anne Sexton's poems are about family life, usually her own. She was born Anne Gray Harvey in Newton, Massachusetts, on November 9, 1928, the third daughter of Mary Gray Staples Harvey and Ralph Churchill Harvey. Anne's father, Ralph Harvey, owned a profitable wool garnetting business and grew very prosperous during the Second World War making blankets and uniform cloth. His family lived in Wellesley, where his father was a banker. Anne's mother, Mary Gray, was from Lewiston, Maine, the daughter of a small-town newspaper editor. Among her ancestors was a governor of Maine.

Anne spent a privileged childhood in large suburban Boston houses staffed with servants. She had two sisters but remembered being very lonely as a child. Her dearest friend was her great-aunt Anna Ladd Dingley ("Nana"), who lived with the family until Anne was thirteen, when Nana "went mad" and was placed in a nursing home.

Anne said she had a boy-crazy adolescence. She graduated from a boarding school, but wasn't much of a student. At age nineteen, she eloped with Alfred Muller Sexton II (nicknamed "Kayo"). During the Korean War, Kayo spent two years in the navy; Anne clerked in a bookstore and did a little professional modeling. Returning home, Kayo took a job as a road salesman for Ralph Harvey's wool business. The Sextons had two daughters: Linda Gray, born in 1953, and Joyce Ladd, in 1955.

Shortly after the birth of their second child, Anne began receiving regular psychiatric treatment for episodes of severe anxiety. One of her doctors suggested that she take up writing as a form of therapy. She was twenty-eight when she began; by age thirty-two she had a well-received book in print, *To Bedlam and Part Way Back*. She went on to publish seven more books of poetry. Two of them were nominated for the prestigious National Book Award; her third book, *Live or Die*, won the Pulitzer Prize in 1967. The one play she wrote, *Mercy Street*, had a successful run off-Broadway in New York at the American Place Theater in 1969. Though her formal education included only a high school diploma and a college extension course or two, by 1973 she had become Professor of Creative Writing at Boston University and had received three honorary doctorates for her poetry. But fame did not cure her ills. Despite great professional success, Sexton remained prey to morbid sadness and dread. She became addicted to alcohol and sleeping pills, which eventually eroded her judgment. Fearful that she was losing her creativity, she committed suicide by carbon monoxide poisoning a month before her forty-sixth birthday in 1974.

Reviewers and critics of contemporary work generally try to assign new writers to categories, to get a handle on them. During Anne Sexton's lifetime she was consigned by reviewers to a hypothetical "confessional school," along with such poets as Theodore Roethke, John Berryman, Delmore Schwartz, Sexton's teacher Robert Lowell, and her friends W. D. Snodgrass and Sylvia Plath. Confessional poetry seemed to constitute a break with poetic tradition, dispensing with the stance of authorial distance that characterized "high poetry" and widening the scope of permissible subject matter to include intimate and disturbing experiences formerly classified as too personal — sometimes too embarrassing — for serious art. Private and taboo subject matter understood in psychological terms gave confessional poetry its distinctive character.

Sexton, like most of the poets labeled confessional, disliked the reductive implications of the term. She considered herself a story-teller. As she nonchalantly told one of her interviewers, "I tend to lie a lot." As a poet, she felt as free as any writer not only to invent characters and situations but to retouch the family portraits she drew from life. Artful correction of the record occurs in such early poems as "Some Foreign Letters," in which she turns her grandparents' genera-tion into Yankee aristocrats; her own childhood receives a New England gothic treatment in "Kind Sir: These Woods," "What's That," "All My Pretty Ones," "And One for My Dame."

Storyteller was Sexton's preferred label for herself even early in her career, when she was still unknown. "I do have a feeling for stories, for plot and maybe the dramatic situation," she wrote the editor of *The Antioch Review* in 1959. "Most poets have a thought that they dress in imagery. . . . But I prefer people in a situation, a doing, a scene, a losing or a gain, and then, in the end, find the thought (the thought I didn't know I had until I wrote the story)." Sexton frequently exercised this preference by adopting a persona, speaking in the first person from the point of view of an imagined character. "Unknown Girl in the Mater-nity Ward," "The Moss of His Skin," "In the Deep Museum," and series such as "The Jesus Papers" illustrate this type.

The more characteristic narrative voice of Sexton's poetry is sear-ingly personal and is *not* dissociated from the author; in fact, it is possible to piece together in Sexton's work a continuous narrative about a character named "Anne." Born into privilege, she is cursed from infancy with fears that mature into a desire to die. "Anne" appears as girl, young wife, emerging and mature artist, and as a broken woman whose rage is directed against herself. Unlike Sylvia Plath's "I," who somewhat resembles Sexton's, this dramatic charac-ter achieves mythic social significance without becoming identified with mythic characters. In Sexton's work there are no allusions to classical literary heroines. Yet "Anne" is possessed by terrifying forces of darkness and prophecy.

Sexton developed her talents rapidly, once she began writing. In retrospect, her career appears to have four distinct phases: apprenticeship; a middle period during which she wrote her two most popular books, *Transformations* and *Love Poems*; the flowering of her originality as a religious writer; and a brief, final period of collapsing rationality.

The poetry of Sexton's apprenticeship (*To Bedlam and Part Way Back* [1960]; *All My Pretty Ones* [1962]) was written under the influence of the writing workshops she attended from 1957 to 1962. Living in the Boston area, Sexton was surrounded by poets at every level of expertise. She had the good fortune to become close friends with Maxine Kumin and George Starbuck, two poets fond of playing the kind of word games that strengthen a writer's mastery of the way sense writhes in the sound of words. In the workshop she attended with Kumin and Starbuck twice a month for almost five years, Sexton tried out many of the traditional forms poets writing in English have developed since the Renaissance. Her first two books are full of subtly patterned stanzas. Sexton had what is known as a "good ear": she rhymed deftly, craftily, and she was a patient, disciplined applicant of the trial-and-error method of revision. During that same period, Sexton attended writing courses taught by Snodgrass and Lowell, and became a close friend of James Wright's. These were well-established poets who enlarged her knowledge of poetic tradition and who helped her gain professional recognition.

By 1962 Sexton was recognized in the poetry world as a major new talent. Then she began working on a play titled *Mercy Street,* and her production of poetry slowed to a trickle. From 1962 to 1965 she wrote many fewer poems than in her workshop days and began composing in looser forms, abandoning her habit of setting up a grid of rhymes through which to sift her associations. A key poem of this phase is "Flee on Your Donkey," which Sexton revised many times during this period. Ostensibly an account of being hospitalized for the sixth time as a mental patient, the poem also suggests frustration with the themes and strategies of her poetry to date.

> I have come back
> but disorder is not what it was.
> I have lost the trick of it!
> The innocence of it!

"Flee on Your Donkey" appeared in *Live or Die* (1966), the volume that won Sexton a Pulitzer Prize. The book echoes with the despair of the mental patient who has ceased to believe in the possibility of recuperation and who has become suspicious of the routines of treatment. ("O my hunger! My hunger!" is a refrain in "Flee on Your Donkey.") Sexton prefaced the book of poems with "due apologies for the fact that they read like a fever chart for a bad case of melancholy." But she ended it with a wishful decision to recover her will to live — or a temporary conviction that she had done so.

In 1969 Sexton finished *Mercy Street*, a play about a suicidal woman seeking spiritual insight into her perplexing psychiatric state — the same material Sexton had worked into the poems of *Live or Die*. (The poem "Consorting with Angels" was written as a monologue for the play's main character, Daisy.) The play required dialogue and action, and intelligence about the interacting subjectivities of a seductive father, an icily distant mother, a teenage daughter, a spinster aunt. Though Sexton never published *Mercy Street*, the impact of writing it was to be found throughout the rest of her work, in the strongly characterized voice with which the speakers of her lyrics make themselves present.

Live or Die was followed by *Love Poems* (1969) and *Transformations* (1971). In the most interesting poems of these books, Sexton would no longer speak as a sufferer of madness but as a survivor of it, confronting and interrogating the conventions of mainstream American culture.

Anne Sexton's love poems do not much resemble other verses that go by this name. Only infrequently do they sound passionate, sentimental, or even tender. The speaker of these lyrics is used to being regarded as a horde of physical attributes and has learned that sex is a performance ("Us"), that flesh is a commodity ("Mr. Mine"), and that the fascinations of romantic love are scripted early in life ("Loving the Killer," "You All Know the Story of the Other Woman," "The Papa and Mama Dance," "Eighteen Days Without You"). Traces of the sexual revolution taking place in the white middle class are to be found in "The Ballad of the Lonely Masturbator," "In Celebration of My Uterus," and "Song for a Lady." In these poems, women dare to explore their own and each other's body with a certain nervous bravado.

The culminating work of this middle phase — which might be characterized as "mad housewife as social critic" — is *Transforma-*

tions, one of Sexton's most popular books. Before its publication, her editor at Houghton Mifflin worried that the book wasn't quite "Sexton" enough. She had become famous as a poet of anguish; that was the persona cherished by readers who identified with her pain and felt validated by her power to find imagery for it. *Transformations* is a book of fairy tales adapted from the brothers Grimm and narrated by the witty voice of a "middle-aged witch." Sexton's retellings expose the moral universe of the fairy tale as exceptionally conservative, rather than radical, in treating its primary though repressed subject matter, sexuality.

In the works that followed her book of fairy tales — *The Book of Folly* (1972) and *The Death Notebooks* (1974) — Sexton's unique spirituality reached effective and moving formulation. "Need is not quite belief," she comments in a poem from *All My Pretty Ones;* but need led her to religion the way madness led her to fairy tales — in search of cultural explanations. God the Father, Mary the Mother, and Jesus the Man are also characters in the stories we tell children about good and evil. In the last years of Sexton's life, when her need was extreme, she consulted these symbols for therapeutic insight, and found them empty of transcendence ("The Jesus Papers"; "Jesus, the Actor, Plays the Holy Ghost"; "The God-Monger"). Father, Mother, and Man were, after all, fundamental social roles; when Sexton wrote of their divine counterparts, she wrote of the pain of separation. For her, no human relationship offered a secure, enduring bond.

Nor did the Christian religion offer Sexton much comfort or hope, at least if her poems are taken as evidence. And yet an unmistakable tone of spiritual peace rises in *The Book of Folly* (1972) and is sustained in the strongest work of *The Death Notebooks.* It emerges from the center of the powerfully expressed death wish these books contain, in such poems as "Going Gone," "The Silence," "The Death Baby." By 1973, Sexton had divorced her husband and had seen her daughters off to boarding school or college. The family home was empty, or peopled with ghosts summoned back to answer final questions. Sometimes the dead returned in the form of ministering angels, or in vivid, restorative dreams (as in "Dreaming the Breasts"). The imagery of these spirit-world poems at their best — the "Angels of the Love Affair" series, the "Furies" series — is surreal and inquisitive. The speaker seems less a personality than a porous membrane through which life streams in syllables. What organizes the hallucinatory flux in these "spiritual" last poems is confidence in the power of words in sequence to *carry* sense, beyond the mind's power to *make* sense. No matter how florid and irrational the simile a mind may form, Spirit resides there: in the architecture of syntax, the irreducible intelligence of metaphor. A poem is like Communion bread placed on a believer's tongue.

Sexton's major testament to such a faith is the sequence of ten psalms titled "O Ye Tongues," modeled on the *Jubilate Agno* of Christopher Smart. The loose theme of the sequence is praise of the mystery of creation, of which Sexton's imagination is a part; its center is a spiritual autobiography that traces back to infancy the origin of her image-making gift:

> For birth was a disease and Christopher and I invented the
> cure.
>
> For we swallow magic and we deliver Anne.

"Anne," the transfer of the poet's being into a name, positions her identity in the place of spirit: language. "O Ye Tongues" is suffused with affection; yet it is quite obviously a "last poem," a farewell that breathes profound, serene acceptance of the world as it is given.

The last book Anne Sexton saw into print was *The Awful Rowing Toward God* (1975); she corrected the galleys the day of her death. The volume has an unpruned quality. Though the uncanny power of similes jammed together was a constant in her work, by 1973 she was apparently unable to develop resonant contexts for inspired lines that yearned to be poems. Equally unfinished — at least by her former ambitious standards — were the poems found in manuscript after her death. In the best of them, she again tapped the strength that was peculiarly her own, "a feeling for stories, for plot and maybe the dramatic situation." Late poems such as "Riding the Elevator into the Sky," "When Man Enters Woman," the "Bestiary U.S.A." series, and "The Horoscope Poems" — these have the seasoned poet's gift of rhythmic economy, and the storyteller's power to disarm and distract.

How will Anne Sexton be read twenty years from now? A hundred? Does she have a permanent place in American literature? The assumption underlying this collection is that her work will endure and that the terms of its endurance will undergo significant revision and expansion.

Sexton was an early spokeswoman in the literature of the women's movement. More than she realized, and more even than the feminists who uncomfortably claimed her realized, Sexton was the modern woman poet who first gave extended voice to issues of female identity. Some feminist critics apologized for Sexton's failure to adopt a political perspective and viewed her primarily as a passive victim. She is the prime example of the problem that has no name, of its partial resolution, and of its possible consequences. But she was among the few women poets of the late fifties and early sixties who, through her transformation from housewife to poet, and through the direct treatment of women's subjects in her poetry, proposed a revolution of intellect and spirit. She will be remembered as a woman poet who embodied and analyzed the position of mid-twentieth-century women as artists, as people in trouble, and as people taking charge.

Arresting imagery was the chief strength of Sexton's poetry. Her language was simple, domestic; but she had a ravishing power of association, which impressed her readers from the beginning. For the jacket of Sexton's first book, *To Bedlam and Part Way Back,* Robert Lowell wrote a blurb that captures the essence of Sexton's style throughout her career. She wrote, Lowell observed, "with the now enviable swift lyrical openness of a Romantic poet. Yet in her content she is a realist and describes her very personal experience with an almost Russian accuracy and abundance."

What Lowell admired was the metaphorical juiciness of Sexton's lines. Lowell called the effect "Russian"; he had been translating Pasternak. It is an agreeable adjective — Russian authors are great-souled, we know that — and one whose implications are worth pursuing. Like the Soviet poets Yevtushenko and Vosnesensky, who were just becoming known in America, Sexton was urgently bent on truth-telling, and what she had to say was quite subversive beneath its unpretentious appeals. And Sexton too expressed her subversive messages indirectly, through metaphors layered with meaning for those who had ears to hear.

A typical poem by Anne Sexton has a "feel" created by slippages along a thread of displacement. Once Sexton abandoned the use of regular, rhymed stanzas — during the period of writing *Live or Die* — she patterned her poems in what might be described as drifts of association. "Flee on Your Donkey" offers some excellent examples. The poem begins as a response to two lines of a poem by Rimbaud (*not* a typical Sexton move), in which she had spotted what she construed to be a pun on her name: *âne* is French for "donkey." "My hunger,

Anne, Anne, / Flee on your donkey," Rimbaud says to her. The flow of association carries her "back to the scene of the disordered senses" (another quotation from Rimbaud): in her case, the return is physical and uncontrollable. She has gone mad again. Though the poem was written and revised over a period of two years, its time frame is the immediate present, each stanza break representing a move in consciousness that turns out to be merely the repetition of an old obsession. The key mood is depressive. Sporadically, a rhyme enters, but it too carries the freight of depression: everything is the same, nothing changes. "This is madness / but a kind of hunger" summarizes the theme of the poem, which is full of gastrointestinal images. Ingestion, digestion, excretion — fundamental and repetitious animal survival — form a sometimes buried axis of reference, as in the lines "I have come back, / recommitted, / fastened to the wall like a bathroom plunger . . ." The implications of this humble simile help us enter the despair of the madwoman: it conveys her rigidity, her self-disgust, the feeling of being seized and rammed violently downward by a sickness out of her control.

The point of reference that organizes this metonymic slide must often be deduced, as in the associations that put "bathroom plunger" in a cluster of stanzas referring also to soup, spitting and gagging, black bananas, and dinner plates. And many of these images are culturally "feminine," drawn from a housewife's occupations and thus unusual in lyric poetry: sheets, aprons, menstruation, spoons, slippers, hot dogs, black bean soup, tomato aspic. Often, the "something" Sexton searches to express through associational references is derived from the privacies of home and of body: "my kitchen, your kitchen, / my face, your face" ("For John, Who Begs Me Not to Enquire Further").

If Sexton's technical achievement is the often brilliant aptness of her metaphors, she is most often praised and admired for the daring of her subject matter. A connection to psychotherapy unites her with several other modern and contemporary poets. But Sexton occupies a privileged place among modern poets in that she created a spacious mythopoesis for the uniquely twentieth-century form of spiritual healing and psychic epistemology represented by psychoanalysis. Some of the mental dynamics uncovered and explored by psychoanalysis are designated by fairly common terms that have entered general usage, such as *conscious* and *unconscious, repression* and *association*. Other psychoanalytic mechanisms and the terms that designate them

— such as projection, displacement, condensation, cathexis, transference, and object relations — are less familiar to both the neurotic and the "normal" personalities whose inner lives and outer behaviors manifest them. In Sexton's poetry, creatively vitalized analogues for these dynamics are often accessible, even revelatory. Her own theoretical readings were restricted to Freud and his followers, but psychoanalytic theory not familiar to Sexton — such as works by Jacques Lacan and Julia Kristeva — can fruitfully be applied to her poems. While Sexton's early poetry was Freudian, her work after *Transformations* became distinctly Jungian in its assumptions about the existence of a collective unconscious, offering a poetic synthesis of the differing developmental emphases within psychoanalysis. That this accomplishment was not the result of a consciously planned program — and it certainly was not — matters little. Sexton recognized that psychoanalytic theory was essentially poetic, linguistic, and metaphorical, and she turned its dry formalism back toward the passionately rich, primary processes from which those formulations emerge, and to which they owe their power. Her poetry speaks with force and value to the theorist, the therapist, the sufferer, and to all those who seek knowledge concerning the dynamics of the psyche.

Sexton wrote the largest, most sustained body of poetry our literature offers on what this culture calls (with its guard up) "mental illness." When the guard is down, we accurately or inaccurately call it being "mad" or "crazy." Because we do not know what madness is, and have never known, and because each historical moment defines the boundaries of mental illness differently, with equal lack of certainty but equally dogmatic conviction, this label is tentative and open to controversy. Was Sexton mentally ill, whatever that means? Emotionally unbalanced? Neurotic? Borderline? Occasionally psychotic? The question is best left to biography, and then to history, which will decide and redecide the question according to the state of the diagnostic art. But for poetic purposes, and in commonly agreed-upon social terms, she spoke of madness, and on behalf of emotionally injured and fragile people. Sexton anatomized the alienated mind and identified with it simultaneously. She served as ritual witness to the inner lives of large numbers of troubled people.

A corollary achievement is Sexton's production of a body of suicide poetry addressed to a culture dedicated blindly to the sanctity of life, and unaware of its own romance with death. The salient, common characteristics of the mad speaker and the suicidal speaker — often but not always the same — are betrayal, abandonment, and guilt. Betrayal is always reciprocal: the suicide betrays the body, the ill person betrays love; but the speaker herself has been betrayed by her beloveds, and by life itself. Abandonment and guilt, on the other hand, function as dualities. The speaker feels she has been abandoned by mother, father, husband, lovers, even sometimes daughters, who reject her or hate her or seduce her or die. But the guilt, even for acts against the speaker, resides within the speaker. She is always responsible — for wanting and needing too much, for losing her balance, for loving insufficiently, for being born female, for being born at all. The punishment for guilt such as this is death.

Perhaps all lyric poetry is elegiac. More specifically and enduringly than most lyricists, Sexton was a poet of loss. The losses are multiple and crucial. They involve the survival of a sense of worth, of definition, of identity, of the validation that one is not only valuable but real. They include the loss of balance and sanity, of loved ones, of childhood. Through her preoccupation with loss, Sexton spoke for the lost child in her collective readership. Nostalgia and celebration suffuse her poetics of innocence, always poised on the moment of integration into experience. Integration is as often experienced as disintegration; the self fused to the point of origin does not always survive the transition.

Finally, Sexton emerges in retrospect as one of our century's most original religious poets, whose work traces the multiple transformations of the ironic doubter, the earnest quester, the desperate believer, the joyous celebrant, the fearless interrogator. Sexton's dismantling of Christian mythology was unprecedented in the poetry of her time. She mocked her deity, dreaming she could "piss in God's eye," but was careful to state that "God is only mocked by believers." Before she became a submissive supplicant, she produced a radical critique of her culture's spiritually impoverished uses of the sacred. Manipulating traditional orthodoxies for happily subversive ends, she rewrote the life of Christ in "The Jesus Papers" and celebrated her own sacraments in "O Ye Tongues." She searched out God in the "private holiness of my hands" and in the remote regions of inner earth, ocean, and sky. Her deities ultimately resided in the "mother, father, I'm made of." She settled, perhaps, for a patriarchal father-god, but she also sought to identify a transcendent mother-goddess she could not name.

Transformation is Sexton's ultimate, final, and collective theme. While transformation always entails the threat of loss, it is also definitive of growth. For every poem that mourns the fragility of the journey from one self, one moment, into another, a different poem (or the same one) celebrates that transition, which can also be toward incarnation, joy, possibility. This is as true of cultural institutions as of individuals in Sexton's terminology. Celebration meets mourning, and nostalgia reaches toward the unknown future, forming intricate contraries in the achievement of this poet.

Sexton's *Complete Poems,* a hefty volume of over six hundred pages, was published in 1981. *Selected Poems of Anne Sexton* is conceived as complementary to that full collection. In choosing poems for inclusion, the editors sought to represent Sexton at the height of her powers. *Selected Poems* spans her career from the era of her premier volume, *To Bedlam and Part Way Back* (including three poems never reprinted after initial publication), to her death in 1974. We have tried to avoid repetition and to select the best works on any given subject, such as suicide, mother-daughter relationships, mental illness, religious questions, and cultural analysis. No fine poem thematically replicated elsewhere in the canon was omitted on the grounds of repetition of subject matter alone; but where a number of poems dealt with a particular theme, the best were chosen.

The series poems, of which there are many in Sexton's work, presented a special problem. Series here are usually represented by individual poems from the group. In selecting the poems, we applied two related criteria: the individual poem had to stand on its own and not require the framework of the series to be comprehensible; at the same time, we tried to represent the impact and intent of the series when possible. Because the series form was among Sexton's most successful vehicles, we include the full texts of two: "Angels of the Love Affair" and "The Jesus Papers," both from *The Book of Folly.*

The length of a poem was inevitably a consideration, but in no case did a long poem — for example, "The Death Baby" or "The Operation" — fail to be included on the grounds of length alone. We might have wished to include additional selections from *Transformations,* if we had had no space constraints, but some of the best are here.

The selection includes no excerpted sections of long individual poems (as differentiated from series poems). While it was tempting to include fine sections or stanzas from long pieces that did not in their entirety meet Sexton's own highest standards, or that suffered from lapses in editing, we did not do so. Thus *The Complete Poems* remains a source not only for Sexton's less distinguished if thematically important work, but also for examples of effective writing not sustained throughout an entire poem.

The selection includes a few poems that were published posthumously, but no effort was made to represent *45 Mercy Street* (1976) and *Words For Dr. Y.* (1978) in proportion to selections from earlier work; the question of quality precludes proportionate representation. But a further issue arises: *The Awful Rowing Toward God* is the last volume that Anne Sexton prepared for press. The status of the two final collections is problematic. The volume *45 Mercy Street* was assembled, but as a hand-corrected, unedited manuscript; on the evidence of earlier volumes, Sexton's revisions, deletions, and additions might have been extensive. *Words for Dr. Y.* was assembled from drafts and poems found after her death and includes work dating as far back as 1960, as recent as 1973.

Much of the writing in these two volumes, and in the few last poems collected in a separate category in *The Complete Poems,* is in rough-draft form and cannot be expected to measure up to even the fairly lax standards Sexton allowed herself in *The Awful Rowing Toward God.* We considered not including any of this work, so that *Selected Poems* would contain only work we can be certain the poet wished to constitute her edited canon. But in employing the primary standards of quality we exacted from the other volumes, we found that some of the late poems hold up as finished pieces.

The resulting collection is ample but not overwhelming. *Selected Poems* represents the range and eloquence of Anne Sexton's poetry from beginning to end.

The editors thank Alicia Suskin Ostriker for reviewing the manuscript of the book. We counted on her critical eye not only for confirmation but for interrogation of our choices. The final shape of this volume reflects her generous participation. Mac Nelson and Norma Hartner also provided support we appreciate. We thank Linda Gray Sexton for permission to include previously uncollected poems.

Chronology

1928   Born Anne Gray Harvey on November 9 in Newton, Mass., to Mary Gray Staples Harvey and Ralph Churchill Harvey.

1934–47   Educated in Wellesley public schools; graduated from Rogers Hall, a preparatory school for girls in Lowell, Mass.

Published poems in school yearbook. Attended the Garland School, a Boston finishing school for women.

1948   August 16: eloped with Alfred Muller Sexton II ("Kayo").

1949–52   Worked in the Boston area: as a model with the Hart Agency of Boston, as a lingerie salesperson, and as clerk at Hathaway House bookstore. Kayo on active duty in Naval Reserve during Korean War. Brief residence in Cochituate, Baltimore, and San Francisco; lived with parents or in-laws during Kayo's absence.

1953   July 21: Linda Gray Sexton born; moved to 40 Clearwater Road, Newton Lower Falls, Mass.

1954   July 15: Anna Ladd Dingley ("Nana"), great-aunt and childhood confidante, died at age eighty-six.

1955   August 5: Joyce Ladd Sexton born.

1956   March: began consulting psychiatrist about anxieties.

July 13–August 3: hospitalized for treatment; children sent to grandmothers.

November 8: attempted suicide.

December: began writing poetry.

1957   Enrolled in John Holmes's poetry workshop at Boston Center for Adult Education. Met Maxine Kumin.

October: first poem accepted for publication.

1958   Scholarship to Antioch Writers' Conference to work with W. D. Snodgrass.

September: began attending Robert Lowell's writing seminar at Boston University.

1959	January: Sylvia Plath joined Lowell's seminar.

1959   January: Sylvia Plath joined Lowell's seminar.

March 1: first public reading, Poet's Theater, Cambridge.

March 10: Mary Gray Staples Harvey died of cancer.

May 19: Houghton Mifflin Company accepted *To Bedlam and Part Way Back* for publication.

June 3: Ralph Churchill Harvey died of cerebral hemorrhage.

August: received Robert Frost Fellowship to attend Bread Loaf Writers' Conference.

December 10: delivered Morris Gray Poetry Lecture at Harvard.

1960   April: *To Bedlam and Part Way Back* published; nominated for National Book Award.

June–July: courses in modern literature with Irving Howe and Philip Rahv at Brandeis University.

1961   Began writing play, *Mercy Street*. Appointed to Radcliffe Institute for Independent Study.

1962   October: *All My Pretty Ones* published; nominated for National Book Award.

November: Levinson Prize from *Poetry*.

1963   May 22: awarded the first traveling fellowship of the American Academy of Arts and Letters.

August 22–October 27: tour of Europe.

1964   *Selected Poems* published in England.

September–March 1965: Ford Foundation grant for residence with the Charles Playhouse, Boston.

December: moved to 14 Black Oak Road, Weston, Mass.

1965   Elected a Fellow of the Royal Society of Literature, London. Received the first literary magazine travel award from the International Congress of Cultural Freedom.

1966   August: hunting safari in East Africa with her husband.

September: *Live or Die* published.

1967   May: awarded Pulitzer Prize for *Live or Die*. Received Shelley Award from the Poetry Society of America.

July: read at International Poetry Festival in London; toured England.

Autumn: taught at Wayland High School, Mass.

1968   June 11: awarded honorary Phi Beta Kappa from Harvard.

July: formed rock group "Anne Sexton and Her Kind."

Taught poetry at McLean Hospital in Belmont, Mass.

1969	February: *Love Poems* published.
	April: Guggenheim Fellowship for work on *Mercy Street*, produced at American Place Theatre, New York City, October 8–November 21.
	June: awarded honorary Phi Beta Kappa from Radcliffe. Began teaching at Boston University and conducting workshops for Oberlin College Independent Study students.
1970	June: honorary Doctor of Letters, Tufts University.
1971	September: *Transformations* published.
1972	Promoted to full professor at Boston University.
	February: *The Book of Folly* published.
	May–June: Crashaw Chair in Literature at Colgate University. Honorary Doctor of Letters, Fairfield University.
1973	Honorary Doctor of Letters, Regis College. Served on Pulitzer Prize jury.
	January: wrote *The Awful Rowing Toward God*.
	March: separated from her husband.
	May 5: *Transformations* in opera version by Conrad Susa premiered by the Minneapolis Opera Company.
	August: lectured at Bread Loaf Writers' Conference.
	November 5: divorce granted.
1974	February: *The Death Notebooks* published.
	March: reading at Sanders Theater, Harvard University.
	October 4: committed suicide by carbon monoxide poisoning.

Early Poems

The Balance Wheel

Where I waved at the sky
And waited your love through a February sleep,
I saw birds swinging in, watched them multiply
Into a tree, weaving on a branch, cradling a keep
In the arms of April, sprung from the south to occupy
This slow lap of land, like cogs of some balance wheel.
I saw them build the air, with that motion birds feel.

Where I wave at the sky
And understand love, knowing our August heat,
I see birds pulling past the dim frosted thigh
Of Autumn, unlatched from the nest, and wing-beat
For the south, making their high dots across the sky,
Like beauty spots marking a still perfect cheek.
I see them bend the air, slipping away, for what birds seek.

An Obsessive Combination of
Ontological Inscape, Trickery and Love

Busy, with an idea for a code, I write
signals hurrying from left to right,
or right to left, by obscure routes,
for my own reasons; taking a word like "writes"
down tiers of tries until its secret rites
make sense; or until, suddenly, RATS
can amazingly and funnily become STAR
and right to left that small star
is mine, for my own liking, to stare
its five lucky pins inside out, to store
forever kindly, as if it were a star
I touched and a miracle I really wrote.

My Friend, My Friend

For M. W. K., who hesitates each time
she sees a young girl wearing The Cross

Who will forgive me for the things I do?
With no special legend or God to refer to,
With my calm white pedigree, my yankee kin,
I think it would be better to be a Jew.

I forgive you for what you did not do,
I am impossibly guilty. Unlike you,
My friend, I can not blame my origin
With no special legend or God to refer to.

They wear The Crucifix as they are meant to do.
Why do their little crosses trouble you?
The effigies that I have made are genuine
(I think it would be better to be a Jew).

Watching my mother slowly die I knew
My first release. I wish some ancient bugaboo
Followed me. But my sin is always my sin.
With no special legend or God to refer to.

Who will forgive me for the things I do?
To have your reasonable hurt to belong to
Might ease my trouble like liquor or aspirin.
I think it would be better to be a Jew.

And if I lie, I lie because I love you,
Because I am bothered by the things I do,
Because your hurt invades my calm white skin:
With no special legend or God to refer to,
I think it would be better to be a Jew.

From To Bedlam and Part Way Back

(1960)

You, Doctor Martin

You, Doctor Martin, walk
from breakfast to madness. Late August,
I speed through the antiseptic tunnel
where the moving dead still talk
of pushing their bones against the thrust
of cure. And I am queen of this summer hotel
or the laughing bee on a stalk

of death. We stand in broken
lines and wait while they unlock
the door and count us at the frozen gates
of dinner. The shibboleth is spoken
and we move to gravy in our smock
of smiles. We chew in rows, our plates
scratch and whine like chalk

in school. There are no knives
for cutting your throat. I make
moccasins all morning. At first my hands
kept empty, unraveled for the lives
they used to work. Now I learn to take
them back, each angry finger that demands
I mend what another will break

tomorrow. Of course, I love you;
you lean above the plastic sky,
god of our block, prince of all the foxes.
The breaking crowns are new
that Jack wore. Your third eye
moves among us and lights the separate boxes
where we sleep or cry.

What large children we are
here. All over I grow most tall
in the best ward. Your business is people,
you call at the madhouse, an oracular
eye in our nest. Out in the hall
the intercom pages you. You twist in the pull
of the foxy children who fall

like floods of life in frost.
And we are magic talking to itself,
noisy and alone. I am queen of all my sins
forgotten. Am I still lost?
Once I was beautiful. Now I am myself,
counting this row and that row of moccasins
waiting on the silent shelf.

Kind Sir: These Woods

For a man needs only to be turned around once
with his eyes shut in this world to be lost. . . . Not
til we are lost . . . do we begin to find ourselves.

— Thoreau, *Walden*

Kind Sir: This is an old game
that we played when we were eight and ten.
Sometimes on The Island, in down Maine,
in late August, when the cold fog blew in
off the ocean, the forest between Dingley Dell
and grandfather's cottage grew white and strange.
It was as if every pine tree were a brown pole
we did not know; as if day had rearranged
into night and bats flew in sun. It was a trick
to turn around once and know you were lost;
knowing the crow's horn was crying in the dark,
knowing that supper would never come, that the coast's
cry of doom from that far away bell buoy's bell
said *your nursemaid is gone.* O Mademoiselle,
the rowboat rocked over. Then you were dead.
Turn around once, eyes tight, the thought in your head.

Kind Sir: Lost and of your same kind
I have turned around twice with my eyes sealed
and the woods were white and my night mind
saw such strange happenings, untold and unreal.
And opening my eyes, I am afraid of course
to look — this inward look that society scorns —
Still, I search in these woods and find nothing worse
than myself, caught between the grapes and the thorns.

Music Swims Back to Me

Wait Mister. Which way is home?
They turned the light out
and the dark is moving in the corner.
There are no sign posts in this room,
four ladies, over eighty,
in diapers every one of them.
La la la, Oh music swims back to me
and I can feel the tune they played
the night they left me
in this private institution on a hill.

Imagine it. A radio playing
and everyone here was crazy.
I liked it and danced in a circle.
Music pours over the sense
and in a funny way
music sees more than I.
I mean it remembers better;
remembers the first night here.
It was the strangled cold of November;
even the stars were strapped in the sky
and that moon too bright
forking through the bars to stick me
with a singing in the head.
I have forgotten all the rest.

They lock me in this chair at eight a.m.
and there are no signs to tell the way,
just the radio beating to itself
and the song that remembers
more than I. Oh, la la la,
this music swims back to me.
The night I came I danced a circle
and was not afraid.
Mister?

Elizabeth Gone

1

You lay in the nest of your real death,
Beyond the print of my nervous fingers
Where they touched your moving head;
Your old skin puckering, your lungs' breath
Grown baby short as you looked up last
At my face swinging over the human bed,
And somewhere you cried, *let me go let me go.*

You lay in the crate of your last death,
But were not you, not finally you.
They have stuffed her cheeks, I said;
This clay hand, this mask of Elizabeth
Are not true. From within the satin
And the suede of this inhuman bed,
Something cried, *let me go let me go.*

2

They gave me your ash and bony shells,
Rattling like gourds in the cardboard urn,
Rattling like stones that their oven had blest.
I waited you in the cathedral of spells
And I waited you in the country of the living,
Still with the urn crooned to my breast,
When something cried, *let me go let me go.*

So I threw out your last bony shells
And heard me scream for the look of you,
Your apple face, the simple crèche
Of your arms, the August smells
Of your skin. Then I sorted your clothes
And the loves you had left, Elizabeth,
Elizabeth, until you were gone.

Some Foreign Letters

I knew you forever and you were always old,
soft white lady of my heart. Surely you would scold
me for sitting up late, reading your letters,
as if these foreign postmarks were meant for me.
You posted them first in London, wearing furs
and a new dress in the winter of eighteen-ninety.
I read how London is dull on Lord Mayor's Day,
where you guided past groups of robbers, the sad holes
of Whitechapel, clutching your pocketbook, on the way
to Jack the Ripper dissecting his famous bones.
This Wednesday in Berlin, you say, you will
go to a bazaar at Bismarck's house. And I
see you as a young girl in a good world still,
writing three generations before mine. I try
to reach into your page and breathe it back . . .
but life is a trick, life is a kitten in a sack.

This is the sack of time your death vacates.
How distant you are on your nickel-plated skates
in the skating park in Berlin, gliding past
me with your Count, while a military band
plays a Strauss waltz. I loved you last,
a pleated old lady with a crooked hand.
Once you read *Lohengrin* and every goose
hung high while you practiced castle life
in Hanover. Tonight your letters reduce
history to a guess. The Count had a wife.
You were the old maid aunt who lived with us.
Tonight I read how the winter howled around
the towers of Schloss Schwöbber, how the tedious
language grew in your jaw, how you loved the sound
of the music of the rats tapping on the stone
floors. When you were mine you wore an earphone.

This is Wednesday, May 9th, near Lucerne,
Switzerland, sixty-nine years ago. I learn
your first climb up Mount San Salvatore;
this is the rocky path, the hole in your shoes,
the yankee girl, the iron interior
of her sweet body. You let the Count choose
your next climb. You went together, armed
with alpine stocks, with ham sandwiches
and *seltzer wasser*. You were not alarmed
by the thick woods of briars and bushes,
nor the rugged cliff, nor the first vertigo
up over Lake Lucerne. The Count sweated
with his coat off as you waded through top snow.
He held your hand and kissed you. You rattled
down on the train to catch a steamboat for home;
or other postmarks: Paris, Verona, Rome.

This is Italy. You learn its mother tongue.
I read how you walked on the Palatine among
the ruins of the palaces of the Caesars;
alone in the Roman autumn, alone since July.
When you were mine they wrapped you out of here
with your best hat over your face. I cried
because I was seventeen. I am older now.
I read how your student ticket admitted you
into the private chapel of the Vatican and how
you cheered with the others, as we used to do
on the Fourth of July. One Wednesday in November
you watched a balloon, painted like a silver ball,
float up over the Forum, up over the lost emperors,
to shiver its little modern cage in an occasional
breeze. You worked your New England conscience out
beside artisans, chestnut vendors and the devout.

Tonight I will learn to love you twice;
learn your first days, your mid-Victorian face.
Tonight I will speak up and interrupt
your letters, warning you that wars are coming,
that the Count will die, that you will accept
your America back to live like a prim thing
on the farm in Maine. I tell you, you will come
here, to the suburbs of Boston, to see the blue-nose
world go drunk each night, to see the handsome
children jitterbug, to feel your left ear close
one Friday at Symphony. And I tell you,
you will tip your boot feet out of that hall,
rocking from its sour sound, out onto
the crowded street, letting your spectacles fall
and your hair net tangle as you stop passers-by
to mumble your guilty love while your ears die.

Said the Poet to the Analyst

My business is words. Words are like labels,
or coins, or better, like swarming bees.
I confess I am only broken by the sources of things;
as if words were counted like dead bees in the attic,
unbuckled from their yellow eyes and their dry wings.
I must always forget how one word is able to pick
out another, to manner another, until I have got
something I might have said . . .
but did not.

Your business is watching my words. But I
admit nothing. I work with my best, for instance,
when I can write my praise for a nickel machine,
that one night in Nevada: telling how the magic jackpot
came clacking three bells out, over the lucky screen.
But if you should say this is something it is not,
then I grow weak, remembering how my hands felt funny
and ridiculous and crowded with all
the believing money.

Her Kind

I have gone out, a possessed witch,
haunting the black air, braver at night;
dreaming evil, I have done my hitch
over the plain houses, light by light:
lonely thing, twelve-fingered, out of mind.
A woman like that is not a woman, quite.
I have been her kind.

I have found the warm caves in the woods,
filled them with skillets, carvings, shelves,
closets, silks, innumerable goods;
fixed the suppers for the worms and the elves:
whining, rearranging the disaligned.
A woman like that is misunderstood.
I have been her kind.

I have ridden in your cart, driver,
waved my nude arms at villages going by,
learning the last bright routes, survivor
where your flames still bite my thigh
and my ribs crack where your wheels wind.
A woman like that is not ashamed to die.
I have been her kind.

Unknown Girl in the Maternity Ward

Child, the current of your breath is six days long.
You lie, a small knuckle on my white bed;
lie, fisted like a snail, so small and strong
at my breast. Your lips are animals; you are fed
with love. At first hunger is not wrong.
The nurses nod their caps; you are shepherded
down starch halls with the other unnested throng
in wheeling baskets. You tip like a cup; your head
moving to my touch. You sense the way we belong.
But this is an institution bed.
You will not know me very long.

The doctors are enamel. They want to know
the facts. They guess about the man who left me,
some pendulum soul, going the way men go
and leave you full of child. But our case history
stays blank. All I did was let you grow.
Now we are here for all the ward to see.
They thought I was strange, although
I never spoke a word. I burst empty
of you, letting you learn how the air is so.
The doctors chart the riddle they ask of me
and I turn my head away. I do not know.

Yours is the only face I recognize.
Bone at my bone, you drink my answers in.
Six times a day I prize
your need, the animals of your lips, your skin
growing warm and plump. I see your eyes
lifting their tents. They are blue stones, they begin
to outgrow their moss. You blink in surprise
and I wonder what you can see, my funny kin,
as you trouble my silence. I am a shelter of lies.
Should I learn to speak again, or hopeless in
such sanity will I touch some face I recognize?

Down the hall the baskets start back. My arms
fit you like a sleeve, they hold
catkins of your willows, the wild bee farms
of your nerves, each muscle and fold
of your first days. Your old man's face disarms
the nurses. But the doctors return to scold
me. I speak. It is you my silence harms.
I should have known; I should have told
them something to write down. My voice alarms
my throat. "Name of father — none." I hold
you and name you bastard in my arms.

And now that's that. There is nothing more
that I can say or lose.
Others have traded life before
and could not speak. I tighten to refuse
your owling eyes, my fragile visitor.
I touch your cheeks, like flowers. You bruise
against me. We unlearn. I am a shore
rocking you off. You break from me. I choose
your only way, my small inheritor
and hand you off, trembling the selves we lose.
Go child, who is my sin and nothing more.

What's That

Before it came inside
I had watched it from my kitchen window,
watched it swell like a new balloon,
watched it slump and then divide,
like something I know I know —
a broken pear or two halves of the moon,
or round white plates floating nowhere
or fat hands waving in the summer air
until they fold together like a fist or a knee.
After that it came to my door. Now it lives here.
And of course: it is a soft sound, soft as a seal's ear,
that was caught between a shape and a shape and then returned to me.

You know how parents call
from sweet beaches anywhere, *come in come in,*
and how you sank under water to put out
the sound, or how one of them touched in the hall
at night: the rustle and the skin
you couldn't know, but heard, the stout
slap of tides and the dog snoring. It's here
now, caught back from time in my adult year —
the image we did forget: the cranking shells on our feet
or the swing of the spoon in soup. It is as real
as splinters stuck in your ear. The noise we steal
is half a bell. And outside cars whisk by on the suburban street

and are there and are true.
What else is this, this intricate shape of air?
calling me, calling you.

The Moss of His Skin

Young girls in old Arabia were often buried alive next
to their dead fathers, apparently as sacrifice to the
goddesses of the tribes . . .

— Harold Feldman, "Children of the Desert,"
  Psychoanalysis and Psychoanalytic Review, Fall 1958

It was only important
to smile and hold still,
to lie down beside him
and to rest awhile,
to be folded up together
as if we were silk,
to sink from the eyes of mother
and not to talk.
The black room took us
like a cave or a mouth
or an indoor belly.
I held my breath
and daddy was there,
his thumbs, his fat skull,
his teeth, his hair growing
like a field or a shawl.
I lay by the moss
of his skin until
it grew strange. My sisters
will never know that I fall
out of myself and pretend
that Allah will not see
how I hold my daddy
like an old stone tree.

Ringing the Bells

And this is the way they ring
the bells in Bedlam
and this is the bell-lady
who comes each Tuesday morning
to give us a music lesson
and because the attendants make you go
and because we mind by instinct,
like bees caught in the wrong hive,
we are the circle of the crazy ladies
who sit in the lounge of the mental house
and smile at the smiling woman
who passes us each a bell,
who points at my hand
that holds my bell, E flat,
and this is the gray dress next to me
who grumbles as if it were special
to be old, to be old,
and this is the small hunched squirrel girl
on the other side of me
who picks at the hairs over her lip,
who picks at the hairs over her lip all day,
and this is how the bells really sound,
as untroubled and clean
as a workable kitchen,
and this is always my bell responding
to my hand that responds to the lady
who points at me, E flat;
and although we are not better for it,
they tell you to go. And you do.

Lullaby

It is a summer evening.
The yellow moths sag
against the locked screens
and the faded curtains
suck over the window sills
and from another building
a goat calls in his dreams.
This is the TV parlor
in the best ward at Bedlam.
The night nurse is passing
out the evening pills.
She walks on two erasers,
padding by us one by one.

My sleeping pill is white.
It is a splendid pearl;
it floats me out of myself,
my stung skin as alien
as a loose bolt of cloth.
I will ignore the bed.
I am linen on a shelf.
Let the others moan in secret;
let each lost butterfly
go home. Old woolen head,
take me like a yellow moth
while the goat calls hush-
a-bye.

The Lost Ingredient

Almost yesterday, those gentle ladies stole
to their baths in Atlantic City, for the lost
rites of the first sea of the first salt
running from a faucet. I have heard they sat
for hours in briny tubs, patting hotel towels
sweetly over shivered skin, smelling the stale
harbor of a lost ocean, praying at last
for impossible loves, or new skin, or still
another child. And since this was the style,
I don't suppose they knew what they had lost.

Almost yesterday, pushing West, I lost
ten Utah driving minutes, stopped to steal
past postcard vendors, crossed the hot slit
of macadam to touch the marvelous loosed
bobbing of The Salt Lake, to honor and assault
it in its proof, to wash away some slight
need for Maine's coast. Later the funny salt
itched in my pores and stung like bees or sleet.
I rinsed it off in Reno and hurried to steal
a better proof at tables where I always lost.

Today is made of yesterday, each time I steal
toward rites I do not know, waiting for the lost
ingredient, as if salt or money or even lust
would keep us calm and prove us whole at last.

For John, Who Begs Me
Not to Enquire Further

Not that it was beautiful,
but that, in the end, there was
a certain sense of order there;
something worth learning
in that narrow diary of my mind,
in the commonplaces of the asylum
where the cracked mirror
or my own selfish death
outstared me.
And if I tried
to give you something else,
something outside of myself,
you would not know
that the worst of anyone
can be, finally,
an accident of hope.
I tapped my own head;
it was glass, an inverted bowl.
It is a small thing
to rage in your own bowl.
At first it was private.
Then it was more than myself;
it was you, or your house
or your kitchen.
And if you turn away
because there is no lesson here
I will hold my awkward bowl,
with all its cracked stars shining
like a complicated lie,
and fasten a new skin around it
as if I were dressing an orange
or a strange sun.
Not that it was beautiful,
but that I found some order there.

There ought to be something special
for someone
in this kind of hope.
This is something I would never find
in a lovelier place, my dear,
although your fear is anyone's fear,
like an invisible veil between us all . . .
and sometimes in private,
my kitchen, your kitchen,
my face, your face.

The Double Image

I am thirty this November.
You are still small, in your fourth year.
We stand watching the yellow leaves go queer,
flapping in the winter rain,
falling flat and washed. And I remember
mostly the three autumns you did not live here.
They said I'd never get you back again.
I tell you what you'll never really know:
all the medical hypothesis
that explained my brain will never be as true as these
struck leaves letting go.

I, who chose two times
to kill myself, had said your nickname
the mewling months when you first came;
until a fever rattled
in your throat and I moved like a pantomime
above your head. Ugly angels spoke to me. The blame,
I heard them say, was mine. They tattled
like green witches in my head, letting doom
leak like a broken faucet;
as if doom had flooded my belly and filled your bassinet,
an old debt I must assume.

Death was simpler than I'd thought.
The day life made you well and whole
I let the witches take away my guilty soul.
I pretended I was dead
until the white men pumped the poison out,
putting me armless and washed through the rigamarole
of talking boxes and the electric bed.
I laughed to see the private iron in that hotel.
Today the yellow leaves

28

go queer. You ask me where they go. I say today believed
in itself, or else it fell.

Today, my small child, Joyce,
love your self's self where it lives.
There is no special God to refer to; or if there is,
why did I let you grow
in another place. You did not know my voice
when I came back to call. All the superlatives
of tomorrow's white tree and mistletoe
will not help you know the holidays you had to miss.
The time I did not love
myself, I visited your shoveled walks; you held my glove.
There was new snow after this.

2.

They sent me letters with news
of you and I made moccasins that I would never use.
When I grew well enough to tolerate
myself, I lived with my mother. Too late,
too late, to live with your mother, the witches said.
But I didn't leave. I had my portrait
done instead.

Part way back from Bedlam
I came to my mother's house in Gloucester,
Massachusetts. And this is how I came
to catch at her; and this is how I lost her.
I cannot forgive your suicide, my mother said.
And she never could. She had my portrait
done instead.

I lived like an angry guest,
like a partly mended thing, an outgrown child.
I remember my mother did her best.
She took me to Boston and had my hair restyled.
Your smile is like your mother's, the artist said.

29

I didn't seem to care. I had my portrait
done instead.

There was a church where I grew up
with its white cupboards where they locked us up,
row by row, like puritans or shipmates
singing together. My father passed the plate.
Too late to be forgiven now, the witches said.
I wasn't exactly forgiven. They had my portrait
done instead.

3.

All that summer sprinklers arched
over the seaside grass.
We talked of drought
while the salt-parched
field grew sweet again. To help time pass
I tried to mow the lawn
and in the morning I had my portrait done,
holding my smile in place, till it grew formal.
Once I mailed you a picture of a rabbit
and a postcard of Motif number one,
as if it were normal
to be a mother and be gone.

They hung my portrait in the chill
north light, matching
me to keep me well.
Only my mother grew ill.
She turned from me, as if death were catching,
as if death transferred,
as if my dying had eaten inside of her.
That August you were two, but I timed my days with doubt.
On the first of September she looked at me
and said I gave her cancer.
They carved her sweet hills out
and still I couldn't answer.

4.

That winter she came
part way back
from her sterile suite
of doctors, the seasick
cruise of the X-ray,
the cells' arithmetic
gone wild. Surgery incomplete,
the fat arm, the prognosis poor, I heard
them say.

During the sea blizzards
she had her
own portrait painted.
A cave of a mirror
placed on the south wall;
matching smile, matching contour.
And you resembled me; unacquainted
with my face, you wore it. But you were mine
after all.

I wintered in Boston,
childless bride,
nothing sweet to spare
with witches at my side.
I missed your babyhood,
tried a second suicide,
tried the sealed hotel a second year.
On April Fool you fooled me. We laughed and this
was good.

5.

I checked out for the last time
on the first of May;
graduate of the mental cases,
with my analyst's okay,

my complete book of rhymes,
my typewriter and my suitcases.

All that summer I learned life
back into my own
seven rooms, visited the swan boats,
the market, answered the phone,
served cocktails as a wife
should, made love among my petticoats

and August tan. And you came each
weekend. But I lie.
You seldom came. I just pretended
you, small piglet, butterfly
girl with jelly bean cheeks,
disobedient three, my splendid

stranger. And I had to learn
why I would rather
die than love, how your innocence
would hurt and how I gather
guilt like a young intern
his symptoms, his certain evidence.

That October day we went
to Gloucester the red hills
reminded me of the dry red fur fox
coat I played in as a child; stock-still
like a bear or a tent,
like a great cave laughing or a red fur fox.

We drove past the hatchery,
the hut that sells bait,
past Pigeon Cove, past the Yacht Club, past Squall's
Hill, to the house that waits
still, on the top of the sea,
and two portraits hang on opposite walls.

6.

In north light, my smile is held in place,
the shadow marks my bone.
What could I have been dreaming as I sat there,
all of me waiting in the eyes, the zone
of the smile, the young face,
the foxes' snare.

In south light, her smile is held in place,
her cheeks wilting like a dry
orchid; my mocking mirror, my overthrown
love, my first image. She eyes me from that face,
that stony head of death
I had outgrown.

The artist caught us at the turning;
we smiled in our canvas home
before we chose our foreknown separate ways.
The dry red fur fox coat was made for burning.
I rot on the wall, my own
Dorian Gray.

And this was the cave of the mirror,
that double woman who stares
at herself, as if she were petrified
in time—two ladies sitting in umber chairs.
You kissed your grandmother
and she cried.

7.

I could not get you back
except for weekends. You came
each time, clutching the picture of a rabbit
that I had sent you. For the last time I unpack
your things. We touch from habit.
The first visit you asked my name.

Now you stay for good. I will forget
how we bumped away from each other like marionettes
on strings. It wasn't the same
as love, letting weekends contain
us. You scrape your knee. You learn my name,
wobbling up the sidewalk, calling and crying.
You call me *mother* and I remember my mother again,
somewhere in greater Boston, dying.

I remember we named you Joyce
so we could call you Joy.
You came like an awkward guest
that first time, all wrapped and moist
and strange at my heavy breast.
I needed you. I didn't want a boy,
only a girl, a small milky mouse
of a girl, already loved, already loud in the house
of herself. We named you Joy.
I, who was never quite sure
about being a girl, needed another
life, another image to remind me.
And this was my worst guilt; you could not cure
nor soothe it. I made you to find me.

The Division of Parts

1

Mother, my Mary Gray,
once resident of Gloucester
and Essex County,
a photostat of your will
arrived in the mail today.
This is the division of money.
I am one third
of your daughters counting my bounty
or I am a queen alone
in the parlor still,
eating the bread and honey.
It is Good Friday.
Black birds pick at my window sill.

Your coat in my closet,
your bright stones on my hand,
the gaudy fur animals
I do not know how to use,
settle on me like a debt.
A week ago, while the hard March gales
beat on your house,
we sorted your things: obstacles
of letters, family silver,
eyeglasses and shoes.
Like some unseasoned Christmas, its scales
rigged and reset,
I bundled out with gifts I did not choose.

Now the hours of The Cross
rewind. In Boston, the devout
work their cold knees
toward that sweet martyrdom
that Christ planned. My timely loss

is too customary to note; and yet
I planned to suffer
and I cannot. It does not please
my yankee bones to watch
where the dying is done
in its ugly hours. Black birds peck
at my window glass
and Easter will take its ragged son.

The clutter of worship
that you taught me, Mary Gray,
is old. I imitate
a memory of belief
that I do not own. I trip
on your death and Jesus, *my stranger,*
floats up over
my Christian home, wearing his straight
thorn tree. I have cast my lot
and am one third thief
of you. Time, that rearranger
of estates, equips
me with your garments, but not with grief.

2.

This winter when
cancer began its ugliness
I grieved with you each day
for three months
and found you in your private nook
of the medicinal palace
for New England Women
and never once
forgot how long it took.
I read to you
from *The New Yorker,* ate suppers
you wouldn't eat, fussed
with your flowers,

joked with your nurses, as if I
were the balm among lepers,
as if I could undo
a life in hours
if I never said goodbye.

But you turned old,
all your fifty-eight years sliding
like masks from your skull;
and at the end
I packed your nightgowns in suitcases,
paid the nurses, came riding
home as if I'd been told
I could pretend
people live in places.

3.

Since then I have pretended ease,
loved with the trickeries of need, but not enough
to shed my daughterhood
or sweeten him as a man.
I drink the five o'clock martinis
and poke at this dry page like a rough
goat. Fool! I fumble my lost childhood
for a mother and lounge in sad stuff
with love to catch and catch as catch can.

And Christ still waits. I have tried
to exorcise the memory of each event
and remain still, a mixed child,
heavy with cloths of you.
Sweet witch, you are my worried guide.
Such dangerous angels walk through Lent.
Their walls creak *Anne! Convert! Convert!*
My desk moves. Its cave murmurs Boo
and I am taken and beguiled.

Or wrong. For all the way I've come
I'll have to go again. Instead, I must convert
to love as reasonable
as Latin, as solid as earthenware:
an equilibrium
I never knew. And Lent will keep its hurt
for someone else. Christ knows enough
staunch guys have hitched on him in trouble,
thinking his sticks were badges to wear.

4.

Spring rusts on its skinny branch
and last summer's lawn
is soggy and brown.
Yesterday is just a number.
All of its winters avalanche
out of sight. What was, is gone.
Mother, last night I slept
in your Bonwit Teller nightgown.
Divided, you climbed into my head.
There in my jabbering dream
I heard my own angry cries
and I cursed you, *Dame*
keep out of my slumber.
My good Dame, you are dead.
And Mother, three stones
slipped from your glittering eyes.

Now it is Friday's noon
and I would still curse
you with my rhyming words
and bring you flapping back, old love,
old circus knitting, god-in-her-moon,
all fairest in my lang syne verse,
the gauzy bride among the children,
the fancy amid the absurd
and awkward, that horn for hounds

that skipper homeward, that museum
keeper of stiff starfish, that blaze
within the pilgrim woman,
a clown mender, a dove's
cheek among the stones,
my Lady of my first words,
this is the division of ways.

And now, while Christ stays
fastened to his Crucifix
so that love may praise
his sacrifice
and not the grotesque metaphor,
you come, a brave ghost, to fix
in my mind without praise
or paradise
to make me your inheritor.

From All My Pretty Ones

(1962)

The Truth the Dead Know

For my mother, born March 1902, died March 1959,
and my father, born February 1900, died June 1959

Gone, I say and walk from church,
refusing the stiff procession to the grave,
letting the dead ride alone in the hearse.
It is June. I am tired of being brave.

We drive to the Cape. I cultivate
myself where the sun gutters from the sky,
where the sea swings in like an iron gate
and we touch. In another country people die.

My darling, the wind falls in like stones
from the whitehearted water and when we touch
we enter touch entirely. No one's alone.
Men kill for this, or for as much.

And what of the dead? They lie without shoes
in their stone boats. They are more like stone
than the sea would be if it stopped. They refuse
to be blessed, throat, eye and knucklebone.

All My Pretty Ones

Father, this year's jinx rides us apart
where you followed our mother to her cold slumber;
a second shock boiling its stone to your heart,
leaving me here to shuffle and disencumber
you from the residence you could not afford:
a gold key, your half of a woolen mill,
twenty suits from Dunne's, an English Ford,
the love and legal verbiage of another will,
boxes of pictures of people I do not know.
I touch their cardboard faces. They must go.

But the eyes, as thick as wood in this album,
hold me. I stop here, where a small boy
waits in a ruffled dress for someone to come . . .
for this soldier who holds his bugle like a toy
or for this velvet lady who cannot smile.
Is this your father's father, this commodore
in a mailman suit? My father, time meanwhile
has made it unimportant who you are looking for.
I'll never know what these faces are all about.
I lock them into their book and throw them out.

This is the yellow scrapbook that you began
the year I was born; as crackling now and wrinkly
as tobacco leaves: clippings where Hoover outran
the Democrats, wiggling his dry finger at me
and Prohibition; news where the *Hindenburg* went
down and recent years where you went flush
on war. This year, solvent but sick, you meant
to marry that pretty widow in a one-month rush.
But before you had that second chance, I cried
on your fat shoulder. Three days later you died.

These are the snapshots of marriage, stopped in places.
Side by side at the rail toward Nassau now;
here, with the winner's cup at the speedboat races,
here, in tails at the Cotillion, you take a bow,
here, by our kennel of dogs with their pink eyes,
running like show-bred pigs in their chain-link pen;
here, at the horseshow where my sister wins a prize;
and here, standing like a duke among groups of men.
Now I fold you down, my drunkard, my navigator,
my first lost keeper, to love or look at later.

I hold a five-year diary that my mother kept
for three years, telling all she does not say
of your alcoholic tendency. You overslept,
she writes. My God, father, each Christmas Day
with your blood, will I drink down your glass
of wine? The diary of your hurly-burly years
goes to my shelf to wait for my age to pass.
Only in this hoarded span will love persevere.
Whether you are pretty or not, I outlive you,
bend down my strange face to yours and forgive you.

Young

A thousand doors ago
when I was a lonely kid
in a big house with four
garages and it was summer
as long as I could remember,
I lay on the lawn at night,
clover wrinkling under me,
the wise stars bedding over me,
my mother's window a funnel
of yellow heat running out,
my father's window, half shut,
an eye where sleepers pass,
and the boards of the house
were smooth and white as wax
and probably a million leaves
sailed on their strange stalks
as the crickets ticked together
and I, in my brand new body,
which was not a woman's yet,
told the stars my questions
and thought God could really see
the heat and the painted light,
elbows, knees, dreams, goodnight.

Lament

Someone is dead.
Even the trees know it,
those poor old dancers who come on lewdly,
all pea-green scarfs and spine pole.
I think . . .
I think I could have stopped it,
if I'd been as firm as a nurse
or noticed the neck of the driver
as he cheated the crosstown lights;
or later in the evening,
if I'd held my napkin over my mouth.
I think I could . . .
if I'd been different, or wise, or calm,
I think I could have charmed the table,
the stained dish or the hand of the dealer.
But it's done.
It's all used up.
There's no doubt about the trees
spreading their thin feet into the dry grass.
A Canada goose rides up,
spread out like a gray suede shirt,
honking his nose into the March wind.
In the entryway a cat breathes calmly
into her watery blue fur.
The supper dishes are over and the sun
unaccustomed to anything else
goes all the way down.

To a Friend Whose Work
Has Come to Triumph

Consider Icarus, pasting those sticky wings on,
testing that strange little tug at his shoulder blade,
and think of that first flawless moment over the lawn
of the labyrinth. Think of the difference it made!
There below are the trees, as awkward as camels;
and here are the shocked starlings pumping past
and think of innocent Icarus who is doing quite well:
larger than a sail, over the fog and the blast
of the plushy ocean, he goes. Admire his wings!
Feel the fire at his neck and see how casually
he glances up and is caught, wondrously tunneling
into that hot eye. Who cares that he fell back to the sea?
See him acclaiming the sun and come plunging down
while his sensible daddy goes straight into town.

The Starry Night

That does not keep me from having a terrible need
of — shall I say the word — religion. Then I go
out at night to paint the stars.

—Vincent van Gogh in a letter to his brother

The town does not exist
except where one black-haired tree slips
up like a drowned woman into the hot sky.
The town is silent. The night boils with eleven stars.
Oh starry starry night! This is how
I want to die.

It moves. They are all alive.
Even the moon bulges in its orange irons
to push children, like a god, from its eye.
The old unseen serpent swallows up the stars.
Oh starry starry night! This is how
I want to die:

into that rushing beast of the night,
sucked up by that great dragon, to split
from my life with no flag,
no belly,
no cry.

Old Dwarf Heart

True. All too true. I have never been at home in
life. All my decay has taken place upon a child.

—Saul Bellow, *Henderson the Rain King*

When I lie down to love,
old dwarf heart shakes her head.
Like an imbecile she was born old.
Her eyes wobble as thirty-one thick folds
of skin open to glare at me on my flickering bed.
She knows the decay we're made of.

When hurt she is abrupt.
Now she is solid, like fat,
breathing in loops like a green hen
in the dust. But if I dream of loving, then
my dreams are of snarling strangers. *She* dreams that . . .
strange, strange, and corrupt.

Good God, the things she knows!
And worse, the sores she holds
in her hands, gathered in like a nest
from an abandoned field. At her best
she is all red muscle, humming in and out, cajoled
by time. Where I go, she goes.

Oh now I lay me down to love,
how awkwardly her arms undo,
how patiently I untangle her wrists
like knots. Old ornament, old naked fist,
even if I put on seventy coats I could not cover you . . .
mother, father, I'm made of.

I Remember

By the first of August
the invisible beetles began
to snore and the grass was
as tough as hemp and was
no color — no more than
the sand was a color and
we had worn our bare feet
bare since the twentieth
of June and there were times
we forgot to wind up your
alarm clock and some nights
we took our gin warm and neat
from old jelly glasses while
the sun blew out of sight
like a red picture hat and
one day I tied my hair back
with a ribbon and you said
that I looked almost like
a puritan lady and what
I remember best is that
the door to your room was
the door to mine.

The Operation

1

After the sweet promise,
the summer's mild retreat
from mother's cancer, the winter months of her death,
I come to this white office, its sterile sheet,
its hard tablet, its stirrups, to hold my breath
while I, who must, allow the glove its oily rape,
to hear the almost mighty doctor over me equate
my ills with hers
and decide to operate.

It grew in her
as simply as a child would grow,
as simply as she housed me once, fat and female.
Always my most gentle house before that embryo
of evil spread in her shelter and she grew frail.
Frail, we say, remembering fear, that face we wear
in the room of the special smells of dying, fear
where the snoring mouth gapes
and is not dear.

There was snow everywhere.
Each day I grueled through
its sloppy peak, its blue-struck days, my boots
slapping into the hospital halls, past the retinue
of nurses at the desk, to murmur in cahoots
with hers outside her door, to enter with the outside
air stuck on my skin, to enter smelling her pride,
her upkeep, and to lie
as all who love have lied.

No reason to be afraid,
my almost mighty doctor reasons.
I nod, thinking that woman's dying
must come in seasons,

thinking that living is worth buying.
I walk out, scuffing a raw leaf,
kicking the clumps of dead straw
that were this summer's lawn.
Automatically I get in my car,
knowing the historic thief
is loose in my house
and must be set upon.

2.

Clean of the body's hair,
I lie smooth from breast to leg.
All that was special, all that was rare
is common here. Fact: death too is in the egg.
Fact: the body is dumb, the body is meat.
And tomorrow the O.R. Only the summer was sweet.

The rooms down the hall are calling
all night long, while the night outside
sucks at the trees. I hear limbs falling
and see yellow eyes flick in the rain. Wide eyed
and still whole I turn in my bin like a shorn lamb.
A nurse's flashlight blinds me to see who I am.

The walls color in a wash
of daylight until the room takes its objects
into itself again. I smoke furtively and squash
the butt and hide it with my watch and other effects.
The halls bustle with legs. I smile at the nurse
who smiles for the morning shift. Day is worse.

Scheduled late, I cannot drink
or eat, except for yellow pills
and a jigger of water. I wait and think
until she brings two mysterious needles: the skills
she knows she knows, promising, soon you'll be out.
But nothing is sure. No one. I wait in doubt.

I wait like a kennel of dogs
jumping against their fence. At ten
she returns, laughs and catalogues
my resistance to drugs. On the stretcher, citizen
and boss of my own body still, I glide down the halls
and rise in the iron cage toward science and pitfalls.

The great green people stand
over me; I roll on the table
under a terrible sun, following their command
to curl, head touching knee if I am able.
Next, I am hung up like a saddle and they begin.
Pale as an angel I float out over my own skin.

I soar in hostile air
over the pure women in labor,
over the crowning heads of babies being born.
I plunge down the backstair
calling *mother* at the dying door,
to rush back to my own skin, tied where it was torn.
Its nerves pull like wires
snapping from the leg to the rib.
Strangers, their faces rolling like hoops, require
my arm. I am lifted into my aluminum crib.

3.

Skull flat, here in my harness,
thick with shock, I call mother
to help myself, call toe of frog,
that woolly bat, that tongue of dog;
call God help and all the rest.
The soul that swam the furious water
sinks now in flies and the brain
flops like a docked fish and the eyes
are flat boat decks riding out the pain.

My nurses, those starchy ghosts,
hover over me for my lame hours
and my lame days. The mechanics
of the body pump for their tricks.
I rest on their needles, am dosed
and snoring amid the orange flowers
and the eyes of visitors. I wear,
like some senile woman, a scarlet
candy package ribbon in my hair.

Four days from home I lurk on my
mechanical parapet with two pillows
at my elbows, as soft as praying cushions.
My knees work with the bed that runs
on power. I grumble to forget the lie
I ought to hear, but don't. God knows
I thought I'd die — but here I am,
recalling mother, the sound of her
good morning, the odor of orange and jam.

All's well, they say. They say I'm better.
I lounge in frills or, picturesque,
I wear bunny pink slippers in the hall.
I read a new book and shuffle past the desk
to mail the author my first fan letter.
Time now to pack this humpty-dumpty
back the frightened way she came
and run along, Anne, and run along now,
my stomach laced up like a football
for the game.

The Abortion

Somebody who should have been born
is gone.

Just as the earth puckered its mouth,
each bud puffing out from its knot,
I changed my shoes, and then drove south.

Up past the Blue Mountains, where
Pennsylvania humps on endlessly,
wearing, like a crayoned cat, its green hair,

its roads sunken in like a gray washboard;
where, in truth, the ground cracks evilly,
a dark socket from which the coal has poured,

Somebody who should have been born
is gone.

the grass as bristly and stout as chives,
and me wondering when the ground would break,
and me wondering how anything fragile survives;

up in Pennsylvania, I met a little man,
not Rumpelstiltskin, at all, at all . . .
he took the fullness that love began.
Returning north, even the sky grew thin
like a high window looking nowhere.
The road was as flat as a sheet of tin.

Somebody who should have been born
is gone.

Yes, woman, such logic will lead
to loss without death. Or say what you meant,
you coward . . . this baby that I bleed.

With Mercy for the Greedy

For my friend, Ruth, who urges me to make an
appointment for the Sacrament of Confession

Concerning your letter in which you ask
me to call a priest and in which you ask
me to wear The Cross that you enclose;
your own cross,
your dog-bitten cross,
no larger than a thumb,
small and wooden, no thorns, this rose —

I pray to its shadow,
that gray place
where it lies on your letter . . . deep, deep.
I detest my sins and I try to believe
in The Cross. I touch its tender hips, its dark jawed face,
its solid neck, its brown sleep.

True. There is
a beautiful Jesus.
He is frozen to his bones like a chunk of beef.
How desperately he wanted to pull his arms in!
How desperately I touch his vertical and horizontal axes!
But I can't. Need is not quite belief.

All morning long
I have worn
your cross, hung with package string around my throat.
It tapped me lightly as a child's heart might,
tapping secondhand, softly waiting to be born.
Ruth, I cherish the letter you wrote.

My friend, my friend, I was born
doing reference work in sin, and born
confessing it. This is what poems are:
with mercy
for the greedy,
they are the tongue's wrangle,
the world's pottage, the rat's star.

In the Deep Museum

My God, my God, what queer corner am I in?
Didn't I die, blood running down the post,
lungs gagging for air, die there for the sin
of anyone, my sour mouth giving up the ghost?
Surely my body is done? Surely I died?
And yet, I know, I'm here. What place is this?
Cold and queer, I sting with life. I lied.
Yes, I lied. Or else in some damned cowardice
my body would not give me up. I touch
fine cloth with my hand and my cheeks are cold.
If this is hell, then hell could not be much,
neither as special nor as ugly as I was told.

What's that I hear, snuffling and pawing its way
toward me? Its tongue knocks a pebble out of place
as it slides in, a sovereign. How can I pray?
It is panting; it is an odor with a face
like the skin of a donkey. It laps my sores.
It is hurt, I think, as I touch its little head.
It bleeds. I have forgiven murderers and whores
and now I must wait like old Jonah, not dead
nor alive, stroking a clumsy animal. A rat.
His teeth test me; he waits like a good cook,
knowing his own ground. I forgive him that,
as I forgave my Judas the money he took.

Now I hold his soft red sore to my lips
as his brothers crowd in, hairy angels who take
my gift. My ankles are a flute. I lose hips
and wrists. For three days, for love's sake,
I bless this other death. Oh, not in air —
in dirt. Under the rotting veins of its roots,
under the markets, under the sheep bed where
the hill is food, under the slippery fruits

of the vineyard, I go. Unto the bellies and jaws
of rats I commit my prophecy and fear.
Far below The Cross, I correct its flaws.
We have kept the miracle. I will not be here.

The Fortress

while taking a nap with Linda

Under the pink quilted covers
I hold the pulse that counts your blood.
I think the woods outdoors
are half asleep,
left over from summer
like a stack of books after a flood,
left over like those promises I never keep.
On the right, the scrub pine tree
waits like a fruit store
holding up bunches of tufted broccoli.

We watch the wind from our square bed.
I press down my index finger —
half in jest, half in dread —
on the brown mole
under your left eye, inherited
from my right cheek: a spot of danger
where a bewitched worm ate its way through our soul
in search of beauty. My child, since July
the leaves have been fed
secretly from a pool of beet-red dye.

And sometimes they are battle green
with trunks as wet as hunters' boots,
smacked hard by the wind, clean
as oilskins. No,
the wind's not off the ocean.
Yes, it cried in your room like a wolf
and your pony tail hurt you. That was a long time ago.
The wind rolled the tide like a dying
woman. She wouldn't sleep,
she rolled there all night, grunting and sighing.

Darling, life is not in my hands;
life with its terrible changes
will take you, bombs or glands,
your own child at
your breast, your own house on your own land.
Outside the bittersweet turns orange.
Before she died, my mother and I picked those fat
branches, finding orange nipples
on the gray wire strands.
We weeded the forest, curing trees like cripples.

Your feet thump-thump against my back
and you whisper to yourself. Child,
what are you wishing? What pact
are you making?
What mouse runs between your eyes? What ark
can I fill for you when the world goes wild?
The woods are underwater, their weeds are shaking
in the tide; birches like zebra fish
flash by in a pack.
Child, I cannot promise that you will get your wish.

I cannot promise very much.
I give you the images I know.
Lie still with me and watch.
A pheasant moves
by like a seal, pulled through the mulch
by his thick white collar. He's on show
like a clown. He drags a beige feather that he removed,
one time, from an old lady's hat.
We laugh and we touch.
I promise you love. Time will not take away that.

Old

I'm afraid of needles.
I'm tired of rubber sheets and tubes.
I'm tired of faces that I don't know
and now I think that death is starting.
Death starts like a dream,
full of objects and my sister's laughter.
We are young and we are walking
and picking wild blueberries
all the way to Damariscotta.
Oh Susan, she cried,
you've stained your new waist.
Sweet taste —
my mouth so full
and the sweet blue running out
all the way to Damariscotta.
What are you doing? Leave me alone!
Can't you see I'm dreaming?
In a dream you are never eighty.

Housewife

Some women marry houses.
It's another kind of skin; it has a heart,
a mouth, a liver and bowel movements.
The walls are permanent and pink.
See how she sits on her knees all day,
faithfully washing herself down.
Men enter by force, drawn back like Jonah
into their fleshy mothers.
A woman *is* her mother.
That's the main thing.

Letter Written on a Ferry
While Crossing Long Island Sound

I am surprised to see
that the ocean is still going on.
Now I am going back
and I have ripped my hand
from your hand as I said I would
and I have made it this far
as I said I would
and I am on the top deck now
holding my wallet, my cigarettes
and my car keys
at 2 o'clock on a Tuesday
in August of 1960.

Dearest,
although everything has happened,
nothing has happened.
The sea is very old.
The sea is the face of Mary,
without miracles or rage
or unusual hope,
grown rough and wrinkled
with incurable age.

Still,
I have eyes.
These are my eyes:
the orange letters that spell
ORIENT on the life preserver
that hangs by my knees;
the cement lifeboat that wears
its dirty canvas coat;
the faded sign that sits on its shelf
saying KEEP OFF.
Oh, all right, I say,
I'll save myself.

Over my right shoulder
I see four nuns
who sit like a bridge club,
their faces poked out
from under their habits,
as good as good babies who
have sunk into their carriages.
Without discrimination
the wind pulls the skirts
of their arms.
Almost undressed,
I see what remains:
that holy wrist,
that ankle,
that chain.

Oh God,
although I am very sad,
could you please
let these four nuns
loosen from their leather boots
and their wooden chairs
to rise out
over this greasy deck,
out over this iron rail,
nodding their pink heads to one side,
flying four abreast
in the old-fashioned side stroke;
each mouth open and round,
breathing together
as fish do,
singing without sound.

Dearest,
see how my dark girls sally forth,
over the passing lighthouse of Plum Gut,
its shell as rusty
as a camp dish,
as fragile as a pagoda
on a stone;

out over the little lighthouse
that warns me of drowning winds
that rub over its blind bottom
and its blue cover;
winds that will take the toes
and the ears of the rider
or the lover.

There go my dark girls,
their dresses puff
in the leeward air.
Oh, they are lighter than flying dogs
or the breath of dolphins;
each mouth opens gratefully,
wider than a milk cup.
My dark girls sing for this.
They are going up.
See them rise
on black wings, drinking
the sky, without smiles
or hands
or shoes.
They call back to us
from the gauzy edge of paradise,
good news, good news.

For Eleanor Boylan Talking with God

God has a brown voice,
as soft and full as beer.
Eleanor, who is more beautiful than my mother,
is standing in her kitchen talking
and I am breathing in my cigarettes like poison.
She stands in her lemon-colored sun dress
motioning to God with her wet hands
glossy from the washing of egg plates.
She tells him! She tells him like a drunk
who doesn't need to see to talk.
It's casual but friendly.
God is as close as the ceiling.

Though no one can ever know,
I don't think he has a face.
He had a face when I was six and a half.
Now he is large, covering up the sky
like a great resting jellyfish.
When I was eight I thought the dead people
stayed up there like blimps.
Now my chair is as hard as a scarecrow
and outside the summer flies sing like a choir.
Eleanor, before he leaves tell him . . .
Oh Eleanor, Eleanor,
tell him before death uses you up.

The Black Art

A woman who writes feels too much,
those trances and portents!
As if cycles and children and islands
weren't enough; as if mourners and gossips
and vegetables were never enough.
She thinks she can warn the stars.
A writer is essentially a spy.
Dear love, I am that girl.

A man who writes knows too much,
such spells and fetiches!
As if erections and congresses and products
weren't enough; as if machines and galleons
and wars were never enough.
With used furniture he makes a tree.
A writer is essentially a crook.
Dear love, you are that man.

Never loving ourselves,
hating even our shoes and our hats,
we love each other, *precious, precious.*
Our hands are light blue and gentle.
Our eyes are full of terrible confessions.
But when we marry,
the children leave in disgust.
There is too much food and no one left over
to eat up all the weird abundance.

From Live or Die

(1966)

And One for My Dame

A born salesman,
my father made all his dough
by selling wool to Fieldcrest, Woolrich and Faribo.

A born talker,
he could sell one hundred wet-down bales
of that white stuff. He could clock the miles and sales

and make it pay.
At home each sentence he would utter
had first pleased the buyer who'd paid him off in butter.

Each word
had been tried over and over, at any rate,
on the man who was sold by the man who filled my plate.

My father hovered
over the Yorkshire pudding and the beef:
a peddler, a hawker, a merchant and an Indian chief.

Roosevelt! Willkie! and war!
How suddenly gauche I was
with my old-maid heart and my funny teenage applause.

Each night at home
my father was in love with maps
while the radio fought its battles with Nazis and Japs.

Except when he hid
in his bedroom on a three-day drunk,
he typed out complex itineraries, packed his trunk,

his matched luggage
and pocketed a confirmed reservation,
his heart already pushing over the red routes of the nation.

I sit at my desk
each night with no place to go,
opening the wrinkled maps of Milwaukee and Buffalo,

the whole U.S.,
its cemeteries, its arbitrary time zones,
through routes like small veins, capitals like small stones.

He died on the road,
his heart pushed from neck to back,
his white hanky signaling from the window of the Cadillac.

My husband,
as blue-eyed as a picture book, sells wool:
boxes of card waste, laps and rovings he can pull

to the thread
and say *Leicester, Rambouillet, Merino,*
a half-blood, it's greasy and thick, yellow as old snow.

And when you drive off, my darling,
Yes, sir! Yes, sir! It's one for my dame,
your sample cases branded with my father's name,

your itinerary open,
its tolls ticking and greedy,
its highways built up like new loves, raw and speedy.

Flee on Your Donkey

Ma faim, Anne, Anne,
Fuis sur ton âne . . . Rimbaud

Because there was no other place
to flee to,
I came back to the scene of the disordered senses,
came back last night at midnight,
arriving in the thick June night
without luggage or defenses,
giving up my car keys and my cash,
keeping only a pack of Salem cigarettes
the way a child holds on to a toy.
I signed myself in where a stranger
puts the inked-in X's —
for this is a mental hospital,
not a child's game.

Today an interne knocks my knees,
testing for reflexes.
Once I would have winked and begged for dope.
Today I am terribly patient.
Today crows play black-jack
on the stethoscope.

Everyone has left me
except my muse,
that good nurse.
She stays in my hand,
a mild white mouse.

The curtains, lazy and delicate,
billow and flutter and drop
like the Victorian skirts
of my two maiden aunts
who kept an antique shop.

Hornets have been sent.
They cluster like floral arrangements on the screen.
Hornets, dragging their thin stingers,
hover outside, all knowing,
hissing: *the hornet knows.*
I heard it as a child
but what was it that he meant?
The hornet knows!
What happened to Jack and Doc and Reggy?
Who remembers what lurks in the heart of man?
What did The Green Hornet mean, *he knows?*
Or have I got it wrong?
Is it The Shadow who had seen
me from my bedside radio?

Now it's *Dinn, Dinn, Dinn!*
while the ladies in the next room argue
and pick their teeth.
Upstairs a girl curls like a snail;
in another room someone tries to eat a shoe;
meanwhile an adolescent pads up and down
the hall in his white tennis socks.
A new doctor makes rounds
advertising tranquilizers, insulin, or shock
to the uninitiated.

Six years of such small preoccupations!
Six years of shuttling in and out of this place!
O my hunger! My hunger!
I could have gone around the world twice
or had new children — all boys.
It was a long trip with little days in it
and no new places.

In here,
it's the same old crowd,
the same ruined scene.
The alcoholic arrives with his golf clubs.
The suicide arrives with extra pills sewn
into the lining of her dress.

The permanent guests have done nothing new.
Their faces are still small
like babies with jaundice.

Meanwhile,
they carried out my mother,
wrapped like somebody's doll, in sheets,
bandaged her jaw and stuffed up her holes.
My father, too. He went out on the rotten blood
he used up on other women in the Middle West.
He went out, a cured old alcoholic
on crooked feet and useless hands.
He went out calling for his father
who died all by himself long ago —
that fat banker who got locked up,
his genes suspended like dollars,
wrapped up in his secret,
tied up securely in a straitjacket.

But you, my doctor, my enthusiast,
were better than Christ;
you promised me another world
to tell me who
I was.

I spent most of my time,
a stranger,
damned and in trance — that little hut,
that naked blue-veined place,
my eyes shut on the confusing office,
eyes circling into my childhood,
eyes newly cut.
Years of hints
strung out — a serialized case history —
thirty-three years of the same dull incest
that sustained us both.
You, my bachelor analyst,
who sat on Marlborough Street,
sharing your office with your mother

and giving up cigarettes each New Year,
were the new God,
the manager of the Gideon Bible.

I was your third-grader
with a blue star on my forehead.
In trance I could be any age,
voice, gesture — all turned backward
like a drugstore clock.
Awake, I memorized dreams.
Dreams came into the ring
like third string fighters,
each one a bad bet
who might win
because there was no other.

I stared at them,
concentrating on the abyss
the way one looks down into a rock quarry,
uncountable miles down,
my hands swinging down like hooks
to pull dreams up out of their cage.
O my hunger! My hunger!

Once,
outside your office,
I collapsed in the old-fashioned swoon
between the illegally parked cars.
I threw myself down,
pretending dead for eight hours.
I thought I had died
into a snowstorm.
Above my head
chains cracked along like teeth
digging their way through the snowy street.
I lay there
like an overcoat
that someone had thrown away.
You carried me back in,

awkwardly, tenderly,
with the help of the red-haired secretary
who was built like a lifeguard.
My shoes,
I remember,
were lost in the snowbank
as if I planned never to walk again.

That was the winter
that my mother died,
half mad on morphine,
blown up, at last,
like a pregnant pig.
I was her dreamy evil eye.
In fact,
I carried a knife in my pocketbook —
my husband's good L. L. Bean hunting knife.
I wasn't sure if I should slash a tire
or scrape the guts out of some dream.

You taught me
to believe in dreams;
thus I was the dredger.
I held them like an old woman with arthritic fingers,
carefully straining the water out —
sweet dark playthings,
and above all, mysterious
until they grew mournful and weak.
O my hunger! My hunger!
I was the one
who opened the warm eyelid
like a surgeon
and brought forth young girls
to grunt like fish.

I told you,
I said —
but I was lying —
that the knife was for my mother . . .
and then I delivered her.

The curtains flutter out
and slump against the bars.
They are my two thin ladies
named Blanche and Rose.
The grounds outside
are pruned like an estate at Newport.
Far off, in the field,
something yellow grows.

Was it last month or last year
that the ambulance ran like a hearse
with its siren blowing on suicide —
Dinn, dinn, dinn! —
a noon whistle that kept insisting on life
all the way through the traffic lights?

I have come back
but disorder is not what it was.
I have lost the trick of it!
The innocence of it!
That fellow-patient in his stovepipe hat
with his fiery joke, his manic smile —
even he seems blurred, small and pale.
I have come back,
recommitted,
fastened to the wall like a bathroom plunger,
held like a prisoner
who was so poor
he fell in love with jail.

I stand at this old window
complaining of the soup,
examining the grounds,
allowing myself the wasted life.
Soon I will raise my face for a white flag,
and when God enters the fort,
I won't spit or gag on his finger.
I will eat it like a white flower.
Is this the old trick, the wasting away,

the skull that waits for its dose
of electric power?

This is madness
but a kind of hunger.
What good are my questions
in this hierarchy of death
where the earth and the stones go
Dinn! Dinn! Dinn!
It is hardly a feast.
It is my stomach that makes me suffer.

Turn, my hungers!
For once make a deliberate decision.
There are brains that rot here
like black bananas.
Hearts have grown as flat as dinner plates.
Anne, Anne,
flee on your donkey,
flee this sad hotel,
ride out on some hairy beast,
gallop backward pressing
your buttocks to his withers,
sit to his clumsy gait somehow.
Ride out
any old way you please!
In this place everyone talks to his own mouth.
That's what it means to be crazy.

Those I loved best died of it —
the fool's disease.

Somewhere in Africa

Must you leave, John Holmes, with the prayers and psalms
you never said, said over you? Death with no rage
to weigh you down? Praised by the mild God, his arm
over the pulpit, leaving you timid, with no real age,

whitewashed by belief, as dull as the windy preacher!
Dead of a dark thing, John Holmes, you've been lost
in the college chapel, mourned as father and teacher,
mourned with piety and grace under the University Cross.

Your last book unsung, your last hard words unknown,
abandoned by science, cancer blossomed in your throat,
rooted like bougainvillea into your gray backbone,
ruptured your pores until you wore it like a coat.

The thick petals, the exotic reds, the purples and whites
covered up your nakedness and bore you up with all
their blind power. I think of your last June nights
in Boston, your body swollen but light, your eyes small

as you let the nurses carry you into a strange land.
. . . If this is death and God is necessary let him be hidden
from the missionary, the well-wisher and the glad hand.
Let God be some tribal female who is known but forbidden.

Let there be this God who is a woman who will place you
upon her shallow boat, who is a woman naked to the waist,
moist with palm oil and sweat, a woman of some virtue
and wild breasts, her limbs excellent, unbruised and chaste.

Let her take you. She will put twelve strong men at the oars
for you are stronger than mahogany and your bones fill
the boat high as with fruit and bark from the interior.
She will have you now, you whom the funeral cannot kill.

John Holmes, cut from a single tree, lie heavy in her hold
and go down that river with the ivory, the copra and the gold.

Consorting with Angels

I was tired of being a woman,
tired of the spoons and the pots,
tired of my mouth and my breasts,
tired of the cosmetics and the silks.
There were still men who sat at my table,
circled around the bowl I offered up.
The bowl was filled with purple grapes
and the flies hovered in for the scent
and even my father came with his white bone.
But I was tired of the gender of things.

Last night I had a dream
and I said to it . . .
"You are the answer.
You will outlive my husband and my father."
In that dream there was a city made of chains
where Joan was put to death in man's clothes
and the nature of the angels went unexplained,
no two made in the same species,
one with a nose, one with an ear in its hand,
one chewing a star and recording its orbit,
each one like a poem obeying itself,
performing God's functions,
a people apart.

"You are the answer,"
I said, and entered,
lying down on the gates of the city.
Then the chains were fastened around me
and I lost my common gender and my final aspect.
Adam was on the left of me
and Eve was on the right of me,
both thoroughly inconsistent with the world of reason.
We wove our arms together
and rode under the sun.

I was not a woman anymore,
not one thing or the other.

O daughters of Jerusalem,
the king has brought me into his chamber.
I am black and I am beautiful.
I've been opened and undressed.
I have no arms or legs.
I'm all one skin like a fish.
I'm no more a woman
than Christ was a man.

The Legend of the One-Eyed Man

Like Oedipus I am losing my sight.
Like Judas I have done my wrong.
Their punishment is over;
the shame and disgrace of it
are all used up.
But as for me,
look into my face
and you will know that crimes dropped upon me
as from a high building
and although I cannot speak of them
or explain the degrading details
I have remembered much
about Judas —
about Judas, the old and the famous —
that you overlooked.

The story of his life
is the story of mine.
I have one glass eye.
My nerves push against its painted surface
but the other one
waiting for judgment
continues to see . . .

Of course
the New Testament is very small.
Its mouth opens four times —
as out-of-date as a prehistoric monster,
yet somehow man-made,
held together by pullies
like the stone jaw of a back-hoe.
It gouges out the Judaic ground,
taking its own backyard
like a virgin daughter.

And furthermore how did Judas come into it —
that Judas Iscariot,
belonging to the tribe of Reuben?
He should have tried to lift him up there!
His neck like an iron pole,
hard as Newcastle,
his heart as stiff as beeswax,
his legs swollen and unmarked,
his other limbs still growing.
All of it heavy!
That dead weight that would have been his fault.
He should have known!

In the first place who builds up such ugliness?
I think of this man saying . . .
Look! Here's the price to do it
plus the cost of the raw materials
and if it took him three or four days
to do it, then, they'd understand.
They figured the boards in excess
of three hundred pounds.
They figured it weighed enough
to support a man. They said,
fifteen stone is the approximate weight
of a thief.

Its ugliness is a matter of custom.
If there was a mistake made
then the Crucifix was constructed wrong . . .
not from the quality of the pine,
not from hanging a mirror,
not from dropping the studding or the drill
but from having an inspiration.
But Judas was not a genius
or under the auspices of an inspiration.

I don't know whether it was gold or silver.
I don't know why he betrayed him
other than his motives,

other than the avaricious and dishonest man.
And then there were the forbidden crimes,
those that were expressly foretold,
and then overlooked
and then forgotten
except by me . . .
Judas had a mother
just as I had a mother.
Oh! Honor and relish the facts!
Do not think of the intense sensation
I have as I tell you this
but think only . . .
Judas had a mother.
His mother had a dream.
Because of this dream
he was altogether managed by fate
and thus he raped her.
As a crime we hear little of this.
Also he sold his God.

Protestant Easter

When he was a little boy
Jesus was good all the time.
No wonder that he grew up to be such a big shot
who could forgive people so much.
When he died everyone was mean.
Later on he rose when no one else was looking.
Either he was hiding or else
he went up.
Maybe he was only hiding?
Maybe he could fly?

Yesterday I found a purple crocus
blowing its way out of the snow.
It was all alone.
It was getting its work done.
Maybe Jesus was only getting his work done
and letting God blow him off the Cross
and maybe he was afraid for a minute
so he hid under the big stones.
He was smart to go to sleep up there
even though his mother got so sad
and let them put him in a cave.
I sat in a tunnel when I was five.
That tunnel, my mother said,
went straight into the big river
and so I never went again.
Maybe Jesus knew my tunnel
and crawled right through to the river
so he could wash all the blood off.
Maybe he only meant to get clean
and then come back again?
Don't tell me that he went up in smoke
like Daddy's cigar!
He didn't blow out like a match!

It is special
being here at Easter
with the Cross they built like a capital T.
The ceiling is an upside-down rowboat.
I usually count its ribs.
Maybe he was drowning?
Or maybe we are all upside down?
I can see the face of a mouse inside
of all that stained-glass window.
Well, it could be a mouse!
Once I thought the Bunny Rabbit was special
and I hunted for eggs.
That's when I was seven.
I'm grownup now. Now it's really Jesus.
I just have to get Him straight.
And right now.

Who are we anyhow?
What do we belong to?
Are we a *we?*
I think that he rose
but I'm not quite sure
and they don't really say
singing their *Alleluia*
in the churchy way.
Jesus was on that Cross.
After that they pounded nails into his hands.
After that, well, after that,
everyone wore hats
and then there was a big stone rolled away
and then almost everyone —
the ones who sit up straight —
looked at the ceiling.

Alleluia they sing.
They don't know.
They don't care if he was hiding or flying.
Well, it doesn't matter how he got there.
It matters where he was going.
The important thing for me

is that I'm wearing white gloves.
I always sit straight.
I keep on looking at the ceiling.
And about Jesus,
they couldn't be sure of it,
not so sure of it anyhow,
so they decided to become Protestants.
Those are the people that sing
when they aren't quite
sure.

For the Year of the Insane

a prayer

O Mary, fragile mother,
hear me, hear me now
although I do not know your words.
The black rosary with its silver Christ
lies unblessed in my hand
for I am the unbeliever.
Each bead is round and hard between my fingers,
a small black angel.
O Mary, permit me this grace,
this crossing over,
although I am ugly,
submerged in my own past
and my own madness.
Although there are chairs
I lie on the floor.
Only my hands are alive,
touching beads.
Word for word, I stumble.
A beginner, I feel your mouth touch mine.

I count beads as waves,
hammering in upon me.
I am ill at their numbers,
sick, sick in the summer heat
and the window above me
is my only listener, my awkward being.
She is a large taker, a soother.
The giver of breath
she murmurs,
exhaling her wide lung like an enormous fish.

Closer and closer
comes the hour of my death
as I rearrange my face, grow back,

grow undeveloped and straight-haired.
All this is death.
In the mind there is a thin alley called death
and I move through it as
through water.
My body is useless.
It lies, curled like a dog on the carpet.
It has given up.
There are no words here except the half-learned,
the *Hail Mary* and the *full of grace.*
Now I have entered the year without words.
I note the queer entrance and the exact voltage.
Without words they exist.
Without words one may touch bread
and be handed bread
and make no sound.

O Mary, tender physician,
come with powders and herbs
for I am in the center.
It is very small and the air is gray
as in a steam house.
I am handed wine as a child is handed milk.
It is presented in a delicate glass
with a round bowl and a thin lip.
The wine itself is pitch-colored, musty and secret.
The glass rises on its own toward my mouth
and I notice this and understand this
only because it has happened.

I have this fear of coughing
but I do not speak,
a fear of rain, a fear of the horseman
who comes riding into my mouth.
The glass tilts in on its own
and I am on fire.
I see two thin streaks burn down my chin.
I see myself as one would see another.
I have been cut in two.

O Mary, open your eyelids.
I am in the domain of silence,
the kingdom of the crazy and the sleeper.
There is blood here
and I have eaten it.
O mother of the womb,
did I come for blood alone?
O little mother,
I am in my own mind.
I am locked in the wrong house.

Walking in Paris

I come back to your youth, my Nana,
as if I might clean off
the mad woman you became,
withered and constipated,
howling into your own earphone.
I come, in middle age,
to find you at twenty in high hair and long Victorian skirts
trudging shanks' mare fifteen miles a day in Paris
because you could not afford a carriage.
I have walked sixteen miles today.
I have kept up.

I read your Paris letters of 1890.
Each night I take them to my thin bed
and learn them as an actress learns her lines.
"Dear homefolks" you wrote,
not knowing I would be your last home,
not knowing that I'd peel your life back to its start.
What is so real as walking your streets!
I too have the sore toe you tend with cotton.
In Paris 1890 was yesterday
and 1940 never happened —
the soiled uniform of the Nazi
has been unravelled and reknit and resold.
To be occupied or conquered is nothing —
to remain is all!

Having come this far
I will go farther.
Your are my history (that stealer of children)
and I have entered you.
I have deserted my husband and my children,
the Negro issue, the late news and the hot baths.

My room in Paris, no more than a cell,
is crammed with 58 lbs. of books.
They are all that is American and forgotten.
I read your letters instead,
putting your words into my life.

Come, old woman,
we will be sisters!
We will price the menus in the small cafés, count francs,
observe the tower where Marie Antoinette awaited her beheading,
kneel by the rose window of Notre Dame,
and let cloudy weather bear us home early
to huddle by the weak stove in Madame's kitchen.
We will set out tomorrow in stout shoes
to buy a fur muff for our blue fingers.
I take your arms boldly,
each day a new excursion.
Come, my sister,
we are two virgins,
our lives once more perfected
and unused.

Menstruation at Forty

I was thinking of a son.
The womb is not a clock
nor a bell tolling,
but in the eleventh month of its life
I feel the November
of the body as well as of the calendar.
In two days it will be my birthday
and as always the earth is done with its harvest.
This time I hunt for death,
the night I lean toward,
the night I want.
Well then —
speak of it!
It was in the womb all along.

I was thinking of a son . . .
You! The never acquired,
the never seeded or unfastened,
you of the genitals I feared,
the stalk and the puppy's breath.
Will I give you my eyes or his?
Will you be the David or the Susan?
(Those two names I picked and listened for.)
Can you be the man your fathers are —
the leg muscles from Michelangelo,
hands from Yugoslavia,
somewhere the peasant, Slavic and determined,
somewhere the survivor, bulging with life —
and could it still be possible,
all this with Susan's eyes?

All this without you —
two days gone in blood.
I myself will die without baptism,
a third daughter they didn't bother.

My death will come on my name day.
What's wrong with the name day?
It's only an angel of the sun.
Woman,
weaving a web over your own,
a thin and tangled poison.
Scorpio,
bad spider —
die!

My death from the wrists,
two name tags,
blood worn like a corsage
to bloom
one on the left and one on the right —
It's a warm room,
the place of the blood.
Leave the door open on its hinges!

Two days for your death
and two days until mine.

Love! That red disease —
year after year, David, you would make me wild!
David! Susan! David! David!
full and disheveled, hissing into the night,
never growing old,
waiting always for you on the porch . . .
year after year,
my carrot, my cabbage,
I would have possessed you before all women,
calling your name,
calling you mine.

Wanting to Die

Since you ask, most days I cannot remember.
I walk in my clothing, unmarked by that voyage.
Then the almost unnameable lust returns.

Even then I have nothing against life.
I know well the grass blades you mention,
the furniture you have placed under the sun.

But suicides have a special language.
Like carpenters they want to know *which tools.*
They never ask *why build.*

Twice I have so simply declared myself,
have possessed the enemy, eaten the enemy,
have taken on his craft, his magic.

In this way, heavy and thoughtful,
warmer than oil or water,
I have rested, drooling at the mouth-hole.

I did not think of my body at needle point.
Even the cornea and the leftover urine were gone.
Suicides have already betrayed the body.

Still-born, they don't always die,
but dazzled, they can't forget a drug so sweet
that even children would look on and smile.

To thrust all that life under your tongue! —
that, all by itself, becomes a passion.
Death's a sad bone; bruised, you'd say,

and yet she waits for me, year after year,
to so delicately undo an old wound,
to empty my breath from its bad prison.

Balanced there, suicides sometimes meet,
raging at the fruit, a pumped-up moon,
leaving the bread they mistook for a kiss,

leaving the page of the book carelessly open,
something unsaid, the phone off the hook
and the love, whatever it was, an infection.

Little Girl, My Stringbean,
My Lovely Woman

My daughter, at eleven
(almost twelve), is like a garden.

Oh, darling! Born in that sweet birthday suit
and having owned it and known it for so long,
now you must watch high noon enter —
noon, that ghost hour.
Oh, funny little girl — this one under a blueberry sky,
this one! How can I say that I've known
just what you know and just where you are?

It's not a strange place, this odd home
where your face sits in my hand
so full of distance,
so full of its immediate fever.
The summer has seized you,
as when, last month in Amalfi, I saw
lemons as large as your desk-side globe —
that miniature map of the world —
and I could mention, too,
the market stalls of mushrooms
and garlic buds all engorged.
Or I think even of the orchard next door,
where the berries are done
and the apples are beginning to swell.
And once, with our first backyard,
I remember I planted an acre of yellow beans
we couldn't eat.

Oh, little girl,
my stringbean,
how do you grow?
You grow this way.
You are too many to eat.

I hear
as in a dream
the conversation of the old wives
speaking of *womanhood*.
I remember that I heard nothing myself.
I was alone.
I waited like a target.

Let high noon enter —
the hour of the ghosts.
Once the Romans believed
that noon was the ghost hour,
and I can believe it, too,
under that startling sun,
and someday they will come to you,
someday, men bare to the waist, young Romans
at noon where they belong,
with ladders and hammers
while no one sleeps.

But before they enter
I will have said,
Your bones are lovely,
and before their strange hands
there was always this hand that formed.

Oh, darling, let your body in,
let it tie you in,
in comfort.
What I want to say, Linda,
is that women are born twice.

If I could have watched you grow
as a magical mother might,
if I could have seen through my magical transparent belly,
there would have been such ripening within:
your embryo,
the seed taking on its own,
life clapping the bedpost,

bones from the pond,
thumbs and two mysterious eyes,
the awfully human head,
the heart jumping like a puppy,
the important lungs,
the becoming —
while it becomes!
as it does now,
a world of its own,
a delicate place.

I say hello
to such shakes and knockings and high jinks,
such music, such sprouts,
such dancing-mad-bears of music,
such necessary sugar,
such goings-on!

Oh, little girl,
my stringbean,
how do you grow?
You grow this way.
You are too many to eat.

What I want to say, Linda,
is that there is nothing in your body that lies.
All that is new is telling the truth.
I'm here, that somebody else,
an old tree in the background.

Darling,
stand still at your door,
sure of yourself, a white stone, a good stone —
as exceptional as laughter
you will strike fire,
that new thing!

Your Face on the Dog's Neck

It is early afternoon.
You sit on the grass
with your rough face on the dog's neck.
Right now
you are both as still as a snapshot.
That infectious dog ought to let a fly bother her,
ought to run out in an immense field,
chasing rabbits and skunks,
mauling the cats, licking insects off her rump,
and stop using you up.

My darling, why do you lean on her so?
I would touch you,
that pulse brooding under your Madras shirt,
each shoulder the most well built house,
the arms, thin birches that do not escape the breeze,
the white teeth that have known me,
that wait at the bottom of the brook
and the tongue, my little fish! . . .
but you are stopped in time.

So I will speak of your eyes
although they are closed.
Tell me, where is each stubborn-colored iris?
Where are the quick pupils that make
the floor tilt under me?
I see only the lids, as tough as riding boots.
Why have your eyes gone into their own room?
Goodnight they are saying
from their little leathery doors.
Or shall I sing of eyes
that have been ruined with mercy and lust
and once with your own death
when you lay bubbling like a caught fish,
sucking on the manufactured oxygen?

Or shall I sing of eyes
that are resting so near the hair
of that hateful animal?
Love twists me, a Spanish flute plays in my blood,
and yet I can see only
your little sleep, an empty place.

But when your eyes open
against the wool stink of her thick hair,
against the faintly sickening neck of that dog,
whom I envy like a thief,
what will I ask?
Will I speak up saying,
there is a hurried song, a certain seizure
from which I gasp?
Or will your eyes lie in wait,
little field mice nestling on their paws?
Perhaps they will say nothing,
perhaps they will be dark and leaden,
having played their own game
somewhere else,
somewhere far off.

Oh, I have learned them and know that
when they open and glance at me
I will turn like a little dancer
and then, quite simply,
and all by myself,
I will fall,
bound to some mother/father,
bound to your sight,
bound for nowhere
and everywhere.
Or, perhaps, my darling,
because it is early afternoon,
I will forget that my voice is full of good people,
forget how my legs could sprawl on the terrace,
forget all that the birds might witness,
the torn dress, the shoes lost in the arbor,

while the neighbor's lawnmower bites and spits out
some new little rows of innocent grass.
Certainly,
I need not speak of it at all.
I will crouch down
and put my cheek near you,
accepting this spayed and flatulent bitch you hold,
letting my face rest in an assembled tenderness
on the old dog's neck.

Self in 1958

What is reality?
I am a plaster doll; I pose
with eyes that cut open without landfall or nightfall
upon some shellacked and grinning person,
eyes that open, blue, steel, and close.
Am I approximately an I. Magnin transplant?
I have hair, black angel,
black-angel-stuffing to comb,
nylon legs, luminous arms
and some advertised clothes.

I live in a doll's house
with four chairs,
a counterfeit table, a flat roof
and a big front door.
Many have come to such a small crossroad.
There is an iron bed,
(Life enlarges, life takes aim)
a cardboard floor,
windows that flash open on someone's city,
and little more.

Someone plays with me,
plants me in the all-electric kitchen,
Is this what Mrs. Rombauer said?
Someone pretends with me —
I am walled in solid by their noise —
or puts me upon their straight bed.
They think I am me!
Their warmth? Their warmth is not a friend!
They pry my mouth for their cups of gin
and their stale bread.

What is reality
to this synthetic doll
who should smile, who should shift gears,
should spring the doors open in a wholesome disorder,
and have no evidence of ruin or fears?
But I would cry,
rooted into the wall that
was once my mother,
if I could remember how
and if I had the tears.

In the Beach House

The doors open
and the heat undoes itself,
everyone undoes himself,
everyone walks naked.
Two of them walk on the table.
They are not afraid of God's displeasure.
They will have no truck with the angel
who hoots from the fog horn
and throws the ocean into the rocks outside.
One of them covers the bedstead.
One of them winds round the bedpost
and both of them beat on the floor.

My little cot listens in
all night long —
even with the ocean turned up high,
even with every door boarded up,
they are allowed the lifting of the object,
the placing themselves upon the swing.
Inside my prison of pine and bedspring,
over my window sill, under my knob,
it is plain that they are at
the royal strapping.

Have mercy, little pillow,
stay mute and uncaring,
hear not one word of disaster!
Stay close, little sour feather,
little fellow full of salt.
My loves are oiling their bones
and then delivering them with unspeakable sounds
that carry them this way and that
while summer is hurrying its way in and out,
over and over,
in their room.

Cripples and Other Stories

My doctor, the comedian
I called you every time
and made you laugh yourself
when I wrote this silly rhyme . . .

> *Each time I give lectures*
> *or gather in the grants*
> *you send me off to boarding school*
> *in training pants.*

God damn it, father-doctor,
I'm really thirty-six.
I see dead rats in the toilet.
I'm one of the lunatics.

Disgusted, mother put me
on the potty. She was good at this.
My father was fat on scotch.
It leaked from every orifice.

Oh the enemas of childhood,
reeking of outhouses and shame!
Yet you rock me in your arms
and whisper my nickname.

Or else you hold my hand
and teach me love too late.
And that's the hand of the arm
they tried to amputate.

Though I was almost seven
I was an awful brat.
I put it in the Easy Wringer.
It came out nice and flat.

I was an instant cripple
from my finger to my shoulder.
The laundress wept and swooned.
My mother had to hold her.

I knew I was a cripple.
Of course, I'd known it from the start.
My father took the crowbar
and broke that wringer's heart.

The surgeons shook their heads.
They really didn't know —
Would the cripple inside of me
be a cripple that would show?

My father was a perfect man,
clean and rich and fat.
My mother was a brilliant thing.
She was good at that.

You hold me in your arms.
How strange that you're so tender!
Child-woman that I am,
you think that you can mend her.

As for the arm,
unfortunately it grew.
Though mother said a withered arm
would put me in *Who's Who.*

For years she described it.
She sang it like a hymn.
By then she loved the shrunken thing,
my little withered limb.

My father's cells clicked each night,
intent on making money.
And as for my cells, they brooded,
little queens, on honey.

On boys too, as a matter of fact,
and cigarettes and cars.
Mother frowned at my wasted life.
My father smoked cigars.

My cheeks blossomed with maggots.
I picked at them like pearls.
I covered them with pancake.
I wound my hair in curls.

My father didn't know me
but you kiss me in my fever.
My mother knew me twice
and then I had to leave her.

But those are just two stories
and I have more to tell
from the outhouse, the greenhouse
where you draw me out of hell.

Father, I'm thirty-six,
yet I lie here in your crib.
I'm getting born again, Adam,
as you prod me with your rib.

Pain for a Daughter

Blind with love, my daughter
has cried nightly for horses,
those long-necked marchers and churners
that she has mastered, any and all,
reigning them in like a circus hand —
the excitable muscles and the ripe neck;
tending this summer, a pony and a foal.
She who is too squeamish to pull
a thorn from the dog's paw,
watched her pony blossom with distemper,
the underside of the jaw swelling
like an enormous grape.
Gritting her teeth with love,
she drained the boil and scoured it
with hydrogen peroxide until pus
ran like milk on the barn floor.

Blind with loss all winter,
in dungarees, a ski jacket and a hard hat,
she visits the neighbors' stable,
our acreage not zoned for barns;
they who own the flaming horses
and the swan-whipped thoroughbred
that she tugs at and cajoles,
thinking it will burn like a furnace
under her small-hipped English seat.

Blind with pain she limps home.
The thoroughbred has stood on her foot.
He rested there like a building.
He grew into her foot until they were one.
The marks of the horseshoe printed
into her flesh, the tips of her toes
ripped off like pieces of leather,
three toenails swirled like shells
and left to float in blood in her riding boot.

Blind with fear, she sits on the toilet,
her foot balanced over the washbasin,
her father, hydrogen peroxide in hand,
performing the rites of the cleansing.
She bites on a towel, sucked in breath,
sucked in and arched against the pain,
her eyes glancing off me where
I stand at the door, eyes locked
on the ceiling, eyes of a stranger,
and then she cries . . .
Oh my God, help me!
Where a child would have cried *Mama!*
Where a child would have believed *Mama!*
she bit the towel and called on God
and I saw her life stretch out . . .
I saw her torn in childbirth,
and I saw her, at that moment,
in her own death and I knew that she
knew.

The Addict

Sleepmonger,
deathmonger,
with capsules in my palms each night,
eight at a time from sweet pharmaceutical bottles
I make arrangements for a pint-sized journey.
I'm the queen of this condition.
I'm an expert on making the trip
and now they say I'm an addict.
Now they ask why.
Why!

Don't they know
that I promised to die!
I'm keeping in practice.
I'm merely staying in shape.
The pills are a mother, but better,
every color and as good as sour balls.
I'm on a diet from death.

Yes, I admit
it has gotten to be a bit of a habit —
blows eight at a time, socked in the eye,
hauled away by the pink, the orange,
the green and the white goodnights.
I'm becoming something of a chemical
mixture.
That's it!

My supply
of tablets
has got to last for years and years.
I like them more than I like me.
Stubborn as hell, they won't let go.
It's a kind of marriage.

It's a kind of war
where I plant bombs inside
of myself.

Yes
I try
to kill myself in small amounts,
an innocuous occupation.
Actually I'm hung up on it.
But remember I don't make too much noise.
And frankly no one has to lug me out
and I don't stand there in my winding sheet.
I'm a little buttercup in my yellow nightie
eating my eight loaves in a row
and in a certain order as in
the laying on of hands
or the black sacrament.

It's a ceremony
but like any other sport
it's full of rules.
It's like a musical tennis match where
my mouth keeps catching the ball.
Then I lie on my altar
elevated by the eight chemical kisses.

What a lay me down this is
with two pink, two orange,
two green, two white goodnights.
Fee-fi-fo-fum —
Now I'm borrowed.
Now I'm numb.

Live

Live or die, but don't poison everything . . .

Well, death's been here
for a long time —
it has a hell of a lot
to do with hell
and suspicion of the eye
and the religious objects
and how I mourned them
when they were made obscene
by my dwarf-heart's doodle.
The chief ingredient
is mutilation.
And mud, day after day,
mud like a ritual,
and the baby on the platter,
cooked but still human,
cooked also with little maggots,
sewn onto it maybe by somebody's mother,
the damn bitch!

Even so,
I kept right on going on,
a sort of human statement,
lugging myself as if
I were a sawed-off body
in the trunk, the steamer trunk.
This became a perjury of the soul.
It became an outright lie
and even though I dressed the body
it was still naked, still killed.
It was caught
in the first place at birth,
like a fish.
But I played it, dressed it up,
dressed it up like somebody's doll.

Is life something you play?
And all the time wanting to get rid of it?
And further, everyone yelling at you
to shut up. And no wonder!
People don't like to be told
that you're sick
and then be forced
to watch
you
come
down with the hammer.

Today life opened inside me like an egg
and there inside
after considerable digging
I found the answer.
What a bargain!
There was the sun,
her yolk moving feverishly,
tumbling her prize —
and you realize that she does this daily!
I'd known she was a purifier
but I hadn't thought
she was solid,
hadn't known she was an answer.
God! It's a dream,
lovers sprouting in the yard
like celery stalks
and better,
a husband straight as a redwood,
two daughters, two sea urchins,
picking roses off my hackles.
If I'm on fire they dance around it
and cook marshmallows.
And if I'm ice
they simply skate on me
in little ballet costumes.

Here,
all along,
thinking I was a killer,
anointing myself daily
with my little poisons.
But no.
I'm an empress.
I wear an apron.
My typewriter writes.
It didn't break the way it warned.
Even crazy, I'm as nice
as a chocolate bar.
Even with the witches' gymnastics
they trust my incalculable city,
my corruptible bed.

O dearest three,
I make a soft reply.
The witch comes on
and you paint her pink.
I come with kisses in my hood
and the sun, the smart one,
rolling in my arms.
So I say *Live*
and turn my shadow three times round
to feed our puppies as they come,
the eight Dalmatians we didn't drown,
despite the warnings: The abort! The destroy!
Despite the pails of water that waited
to drown them, to pull them down like stones,
they came, each one headfirst,
blowing bubbles the color of cataract-blue
and fumbling for the tiny tits.
Just last week, eight Dalmatians,
$3/4$ of a lb., lined up like cord wood
each
like a
birch tree.
I promise to love more if they come,

because in spite of cruelty
and the stuffed railroad cars for the ovens,
I am not what I expected. Not an Eichmann.
The poison just didn't take.
So I won't hang around in my hospital shift,
repeating The Black Mass and all of it.
I say *Live, Live* because of the sun,
the dream, the excitable gift.

From Love Poems

(1969)

The Breast

This is the key to it.
This is the key to everything.
Preciously.

I am worse than the gamekeeper's children,
picking for dust and bread.
Here I am drumming up perfume.

Let me go down on your carpet,
your straw mattress — whatever's at hand
because the child in me is dying, dying.

It is not that I am cattle to be eaten.
It is not that I am some sort of street.
But your hands found me like an architect.

Jugful of milk! It was yours years ago
when I lived in the valley of my bones,
bones dumb in the swamp. Little playthings.

A xylophone maybe with skin
stretched over it awkwardly.
Only later did it become something real.

Later I measured my size against movie stars.
I didn't measure up. Something between
my shoulders was there. But never enough.

Sure, there was a meadow,
but no young men singing the truth.
Nothing to tell truth by.

Ignorant of men I lay next to my sisters
and rising out of the ashes I cried
my sex will be transfixed!

Now I am your mother, your daughter,
your brand new thing — a snail, a nest.
I am alive when your fingers are.

I wear silk — the cover to uncover —
because silk is what I want you to think of.
But I dislike the cloth. It is too stern.

So tell me anything but track me like a climber
for here is the eye, here is the jewel,
here is the excitement the nipple learns.

I am unbalanced — but I am not mad with snow.
I am mad the way young girls are mad,
with an offering, an offering . . .

I burn the way money burns.

In Celebration of My Uterus

Everyone in me is a bird.
I am beating all my wings.
They wanted to cut you out
but they will not.
They said you were immeasurably empty
but you are not.
They said you were sick unto dying
but they were wrong.
You are singing like a school girl.
You are not torn.

Sweet weight,
in celebration of the woman I am
and of the soul of the woman I am
and of the central creature and its delight
I sing for you. I dare to live.
Hello, spirit. Hello, cup.
Fasten, cover. Cover that does contain.
Hello to the soil of the fields.
Welcome, roots.

Each cell has a life.
There is enough here to please a nation.
It is enough that the populace own these goods.
Any person, any commonwealth would say of it,
"It is good this year that we may plant again
and think forward to a harvest.
A blight had been forecast and has been cast out."
Many women are singing together of this:
one is in a shoe factory cursing the machine,
one is at the aquarium tending a seal,
one is dull at the wheel of her Ford,
one is at the toll gate collecting,
one is tying the cord of a calf in Arizona,
one is straddling a cello in Russia,

one is shifting pots on the stove in Egypt,
one is painting her bedroom walls moon color,
one is dying but remembering a breakfast,
one is stretching on her mat in Thailand,
one is wiping the ass of her child,
one is staring out the window of a train
in the middle of Wyoming and one is
anywhere and some are everywhere and all
seem to be singing, although some can not
sing a note.

Sweet weight,
in celebration of the woman I am
let me carry a ten-foot scarf,
let me drum for the nineteen-year-olds,
let me carry bowls for the offering
(if that is my part).
Let me study the cardiovascular tissue,
let me examine the angular distance of meteors,
let me suck on the stems of flowers
(if that is my part).
Let me make certain tribal figures
(if that is my part).
For this thing the body needs
let me sing
for the supper,
for the kissing,
for the correct
yes.

Loving the Killer

Today is the day they shipped
home our summer in two crates
and tonight is All Hallows Eve
and today you tell me the oak leaves
outside your office window will
outlast the New England winter.
But then, love is where our summer
was.

Though I never touched a rifle,
love was under the canvas,
deep in the bush of Tanzania.
Though I only carried a camera,
love came after the gun,
after the kill,
after the martinis and
the eating of the kill.
While Saedi, a former cannibal,
served from the left
in his white gown and red fez,
I vomited behind the dining tent.
Love where the hyena laughed
in the middle of nowhere
except the equator. Love!

Yet today our dog is full
of our dead dog's spirit
and limps on three legs,
holding up the dead dog's paw.
Though the house is full of
candy bars the wasted ghost
of my parents is poking
the keyhole, rubbing the bedpost.
Also the ghost of your father,
who was killed outright.

Tonight we will argue and shout,
"My loss is greater than yours!
My pain is more valuable!"

Today they shipped home our summer
in two crates wrapped in brown
waxed paper and sewn in burlap.
The first crate holds our personal
effects, sweaty jackets, 3 lb. boots
from the hold of the S.S. MORMACRIO
by way of Mombassa, Dar es Salaam,
Tanga, Lourence Marques and Zanzibar,
through customs along with the other
merchandise: ash blonde sisal like
horse's tails, and hairy strings,
bales of grease wool from the auctions
at Cape Town and something else. Bones!

Bones piled up like coal, animal bones
shaped like golf balls, school pencils,
fingers and noses. Oh my Nazi,
with your S.S. sky-blue eye —
I am no different from Emily Goering.
Emily Goering recently said she
thought the concentration camps
were for the re-education of Jews
and Communists. She thought!
So far the continents stay on the map
but there is always a new method.

The other crate we own is dead.
Bones and skins from Hold #1
going to New York for curing and
mounting. We have not touched these
skulls since a Friday in Arusha where
skulls lay humbly beside the Land Rover,
flies still sucking on eye pits,
all in a row, head by head,
beside the ivory that cost more

than your life. The wildebeest
skull, the eland skull, the Grant's
skull, the Thomson's skull, the impala
skull and the hartebeest skull,
on and on to New York along with
the skins of zebras and leopards.

And tonight our skins, our bones,
that have survived our fathers,
will meet, delicate in the hold,
fastened together in an intricate
lock. Then one of us will shout,
"My need is more desperate!" and
I will eat you slowly with kisses
even though the killer in you
has gotten out.

For My Lover, Returning to His Wife

She is all there.
She was melted carefully down for you
and cast up from your childhood,
cast up from your one hundred favorite aggies.

She has always been there, my darling.
She is, in fact, exquisite.
Fireworks in the dull middle of February
and as real as a cast-iron pot.

Let's face it, I have been momentary.
A luxury. A bright red sloop in the harbor.
My hair rising like smoke from the car window.
Littleneck clams out of season.
She is more than that. She is your have to have,
has grown you your practical your tropical growth.
This is not an experiment. She is all harmony.
She sees to oars and oarlocks for the dinghy,

has placed wild flowers at the window at breakfast,
sat by the potter's wheel at midday,
set forth three children under the moon,
three cherubs drawn by Michelangelo,

done this with her legs spread out
in the terrible months in the chapel.
If you glance up, the children are there
like delicate balloons resting on the ceiling.

She has also carried each one down the hall
after supper, their heads privately bent,
two legs protesting, person to person,
her face flushed with a song and their little sleep.

I give you back your heart.
I give you permission —

for the fuse inside her, throbbing
angrily in the dirt, for the bitch in her
and the burying of her wound —
for the burying of her small red wound alive —

for the pale flickering flare under her ribs,
for the drunken sailor who waits in her left pulse,
for the mother's knee, for the stockings,
for the garter belt, for the call —

the curious call
when you will burrow in arms and breasts
and tug at the orange ribbon in her hair
and answer the call, the curious call.

She is so naked and singular.
She is the sum of yourself and your dream.
Climb her like a monument, step after step.
She is solid.

As for me, I am a watercolor.
I wash off.

It Is a Spring Afternoon

Everything here is yellow and green.
Listen to its throat, its earthskin,
the bone dry voices of the peepers
as they throb like advertisements.
The small animals of the woods
are carrying their deathmasks
into a narrow winter cave.
The scarecrow has plucked out
his two eyes like diamonds
and walked into the village.
The general and the postman
have taken off their packs.
This has all happened before
but nothing here is obsolete.
Everything here is possible.

Because of this
perhaps a young girl has laid down
her winter clothes and has casually
placed herself upon a tree limb
that hangs over a pool in the river.
She has been poured out onto the limb,
low above the houses of the fishes
as they swim in and out of her reflection
and up and down the stairs of her legs.
Her body carries clouds all the way home.
She is overlooking her watery face
in the river where blind men
come to bathe at midday.

Because of this
the ground, that winter nightmare,
has cured its sores and burst
with green birds and vitamins.
Because of this
the trees turn in their trenches
and hold up little rain cups
by their slender fingers.
Because of this
a woman stands by her stove
singing and cooking flowers.
Everything here is yellow and green.

Surely spring will allow
a girl without a stitch on
to turn softly in her sunlight
and not be afraid of her bed.
She has already counted seven
blossoms in her green green mirror.
Two rivers combine beneath her.
The face of the child wrinkles
in the water and is gone forever.
The woman is all that can be seen
in her animal loveliness.
Her cherished and obstinate skin
lies deeply under the watery tree.
Everything is altogether possible
and the blind men can also see.

Just Once

Just once I knew what life was for.
In Boston, quite suddenly, I understood;
walked there along the Charles River,
watched the lights copying themselves,
all neoned and strobe-hearted, opening
their mouths as wide as opera singers;
counted the stars, my little campaigners,
my scar daisies, and knew that I walked my love
on the night green side of it and cried
my heart to the eastbound cars and cried
my heart to the westbound cars and took
my truth across a small humped bridge
and hurried my truth, the charm of it, home
and hoarded these constants into morning
only to find them gone.

You All Know the Story
of the Other Woman

It's a little Walden.
She is private in her breathbed
as his body takes off and flies,
flies straight as an arrow.
But it's a bad translation.
Daylight is nobody's friend.
God comes in like a landlord
and flashes on his brassy lamp.
Now she is just so-so.
He puts his bones back on,
turning the clock back an hour.
She knows flesh, that skin balloon,
the unbound limbs, the boards,
the roof, the removable roof.
She is his selection, part time.
You know the story too! Look,
when it is over he places her,
like a phone, back on the hook.

The Ballad of the Lonely Masturbator

The end of the affair is always death.
She's my workshop. Slippery eye,
out of the tribe of myself my breath
finds you gone. I horrify
those who stand by. I am fed.
At night, alone, I marry the bed.

Finger to finger, now she's mine.
She's not too far. She's my encounter.
I beat her like a bell. I recline
in the bower where you used to mount her.
You borrowed me on the flowered spread.
At night, alone, I marry the bed.

Take for instance this night, my love,
that every single couple puts together
with a joint overturning, beneath, above,
the abundant two on sponge and feather,
kneeling and pushing, head to head.
At night, alone, I marry the bed.

I break out of my body this way,
an annoying miracle. Could I
put the dream market on display?
I am spread out. I crucify.
My little plum is what you said.
At night, alone, I marry the bed.

Then my black-eyed rival came.
The lady of water, rising on the beach,
a piano at her fingertips, shame
on her lips and a flute's speech.
And I was the knock-kneed broom instead.
At night, alone, I marry the bed.

She took you the way a woman takes
a bargain dress off the rack
and I broke the way a stone breaks.
I give back your books and fishing tack.
Today's paper says that you are wed.
At night, alone, I marry the bed.

The boys and girls are one tonight.
They unbutton blouses. They unzip flies.
They take off shoes. They turn off the light.
The glimmering creatures are full of lies.
They are eating each other. They are overfed.
At night, alone, I marry the bed.

The Papa and Mama Dance

Taking into consideration all your loveliness,
why can't you burn your bootsoles and your
draft card? How can you sit there saying yes
to war? You'll be a pauper when you die, sore
boy. Dead, while I still live at our address.
Oh my brother, why do you keep making plans
when I am at seizures of hearts and hands?
Come dance the dance, the Papa-Mama dance;
bring costumes from the suitcase pasted *Ile de France,*
the S.S. *Gripsholm.* Papa's London Harness case
he took abroad and kept in our attic laced
with old leather straps for storage and his
scholar's robes, black licorice — that metamorphosis
with its crimson hood. Remember we played costume —
bride black and black, black, black the groom?

Taking into consideration all your loveliness,
the mad hours where once we danced on the sofa
screaming Papa, Papa, Papa, me in my dress,
my nun's habit and you black as a hammer, a bourgeois
priest who kept leaping and leaping and leaping,
Oh brother, Mr. Gunman, why were you weeping,
inventing curses for your sister's pink, pink ear?
Taking aim and then, as usual, being sincere,
saying something dangerous, something egg-spotted
like *I love you,* ignoring the room where we danced,
ignoring the gin that could get us honestly potted,
and crying Mama, Mama, Mama, that old romance:
I tell you the dances we had were really enough,
your hands on my breast and all that sort of stuff.

Remember the yellow leaves that October day
when we married the tree hut and I didn't go away?
Now I sit here burying the attic and all of your
loveliness. If I jump on the sofa you just sit
in the corner and then you just bang on the door.
YOU WON'T REMEMBER! Yes, Mr. Gunman, that's it!
Isn't the attic familiar? Doesn't the season
trample your mind? War, you say. War, you reason.
Please Mr. Gunman, dance one more, commenting
on costumes, holding them to your breast, lamenting
our black love and putting on that Papa dress.
Papa and Mama did so. Can we do less?

Us

I was wrapped in black
fur and white fur and
you undid me and then
you placed me in gold light
and then you crowned me,
while snow fell outside
the door in diagonal darts.
While a ten-inch snow
came down like stars
in small calcium fragments,
we were in our own bodies
(that room that will bury us)
and you were in my body
(that room that will outlive us)
and at first I rubbed your
feet dry with a towel
because I was your slave
and then you called me princess.
Princess!

Oh then
I stood up in my gold skin
and I beat down the psalms
and I beat down the clothes
and you undid the bridle
and you undid the reins
and I undid the buttons,
the bones, the confusions,
the New England postcards,
the January ten o'clock night,
and we rose up like wheat,
acre after acre of gold,
and we harvested,
we harvested.

Mr. Mine

Notice how he has numbered the blue veins
in my breast. Moreover there are ten freckles.
Now he goes left. Now he goes right.
He is building a city, a city of flesh.
He's an industrialist. He has starved in cellars
and, ladies and gentlemen, he's been broken by iron,
by the blood, by the metal, by the triumphant
iron of his mother's death. But he begins again.
Now he constructs me. He is consumed by the city.
From the glory of boards he has built me up.
From the wonder of concrete he has molded me.
He has given me six hundred street signs.
The time I was dancing he built a museum.
He built ten blocks when I moved on the bed.
He constructed an overpass when I left.
I gave him flowers and he built an airport.
For traffic lights he handed out red and green
lollipops. Yet in my heart I am go children slow.

Song for a Lady

On the day of breasts and small hips
the window pocked with bad rain,
rain coming on like a minister,
we coupled, so sane and insane.
We lay like spoons while the sinister
rain dropped like flies on our lips
and our glad eyes and our small hips.

"The room is so cold with rain," you said
and you, feminine you, with your flower
said novenas to my ankles and elbows.
You are a national product and power.
Oh my swan, my drudge, my dear wooly rose,
even a notary would notarize our bed
as you knead me and I rise like bread.

From Eighteen Days Without You

I slept last night
under a bird's shadow
dreaming of nuthatches at the feeder,
jailed to its spine, jailed right
down to the toes, waiting for slow
death in the hateful December snow.
Mother's death came in the spotlight
and mother slamming the door when I need her
and you at the door yesterday,
you at the loss, grown white,
saying what lovers say.

But in my dream
you were a weird stone man
who sleepwalked in, whose features did not change,
your mouth sewn like a seam,
a dressmaker's dummy who began
without legs and a caved-in waist, my old puritan.
You were all muslin, a faded cream
and I put you in six rooms to rearrange
your doors and your thread popped and spoke,
ripping out an uncovered scream
from which I awoke.

Then I took a pill to sleep again
and I was a criminal in solitary,
both cripple and crook
who had picked ruby eyes from men.
One-legged I became and then
you dragged me off by your Nazi hook.
I was the piece of bad meat they made you carry.
I was bruised. You could not miss.
Dreaming gives one such bad luck
and I had ordered this.

Then I think of you in bed,
your tongue half chocolate, half ocean,
of the houses that you swing into,
of the steel wool hair on your head,
of your persistent hands and then
how we gnaw at the barrier because we are two.

How you come and take my blood cup
and link me together and take my brine.
We are bare. We are stripped to the bone
and we swim in tandem and go up and up
the river, the identical river called Mine
and we enter together. No one's alone.

DECEMBER 18TH

Swift boomerang, come get!
I am delicate. You've been gone.
The losing has hurt me some, yet
I must bend for you. See me arch. I'm turned on.
My eyes are lawn-colored, my hair brunette.

Kiss the package, Mr. Bind!
Yes? Would you consider hurling yourself
upon me, rigorous but somehow kind?
I am laid out like paper on your cabin kitchen shelf.
So draw me a breast. I like to be underlined.

Look, lout! Say yes!
Draw me like a child. I shall need
merely two round eyes and a small kiss.
A small o. Two earrings would be nice. Then proceed
to the shoulder. You may pause at this.

Catch me. I'm your disease.
Please go slow all along the torso

drawing beads and mouths and trees
and o's, a little *graffiti* and a small *hello*
for I grab, I nibble, I lift, I please.

Draw me good, draw me warm.
Bring me your raw-boned wrist and your
strange, Mr. Bind, strange stubborn horn.
Darling, bring with this an hour of undulations, for
this is the music for which I was born.

Lock in! Be alert, my acrobat
and I will be soft wood and you the nail
and we will make fiery ovens for Jack Sprat
and you will hurl yourself into my tiny jail
and we will take a supper together and that
will be that.

From Transformations

(1971)

Snow White and the Seven Dwarfs

No matter what life you lead
the virgin is a lovely number:
cheeks as fragile as cigarette paper,
arms and legs made of Limoges,
lips like Vin Du Rhône,
rolling her china-blue doll eyes
open and shut.
Open to say,
Good Day Mama,
and shut for the thrust
of the unicorn.
She is unsoiled.
She is as white as a bonefish.

Once there was a lovely virgin
called Snow White.
Say she was thirteen.
Her stepmother,
a beauty in her own right,
though eaten, of course, by age,
would hear of no beauty surpassing her own.
Beauty is a simple passion,
but, oh my friends, in the end
you will dance the fire dance in iron shoes.
The stepmother had a mirror to which she referred —
something like the weather forecast —
a mirror that proclaimed
the one beauty of the land.
She would ask,
Looking glass upon the wall,
who is fairest of us all?
And the mirror would reply,
You are fairest of us all.
Pride pumped in her like poison.

Suddenly one day the mirror replied,
Queen, you are full fair, 'tis true,
but Snow White is fairer than you.
Until that moment Snow White
had been no more important
than a dust mouse under the bed.
But now the queen saw brown spots on her hand
and four whiskers over her lip
so she condemned Snow White
to be hacked to death.
Bring me her heart, she said to the hunter,
and I will salt it and eat it.
The hunter, however, let his prisoner go
and brought a boar's heart back to the castle.
The queen chewed it up like a cube steak.
Now I am fairest, she said,
lapping her slim white fingers.

Snow White walked in the wildwood
for weeks and weeks.
At each turn there were twenty doorways
and at each stood a hungry wolf,
his tongue lolling out like a worm.
The birds called out lewdly,
talking like pink parrots,
and the snakes hung down in loops,
each a noose for her sweet white neck.
On the seventh week
she came to the seventh mountain
and there she found the dwarf house.
It was as droll as a honeymoon cottage
and completely equipped with
seven beds, seven chairs, seven forks
and seven chamber pots.
Snow White ate seven chicken livers
and lay down, at last, to sleep.

The dwarfs, those little hot dogs,
walked three times around Snow White,
the sleeping virgin. They were wise
and wattled like small czars.
Yes. It's a good omen,
they said, and will bring us luck.
They stood on tiptoes to watch
Snow White wake up. She told them
about the mirror and the killer-queen
and they asked her to stay and keep house.
Beware of your stepmother,
they said.
Soon she will know you are here.
While we are away in the mines
during the day, you must not
open the door.

Looking glass upon the wall . . .
The mirror told
and so the queen dressed herself in rags
and went out like a peddler to trap Snow White.
She went across seven mountains.
She came to the dwarf house
and Snow White opened the door
and bought a bit of lacing.
The queen fastened it tightly
around her bodice,
as tight as an Ace bandage,
so tight that Snow White swooned.
She lay on the floor, a plucked daisy.
When the dwarfs came home they undid the lace
and she revived miraculously.
She was as full of life as soda pop.
Beware of your stepmother,
they said.
She will try once more.

Looking glass upon the wall . . .
Once more the mirror told
and once more the queen dressed in rags
and once more Snow White opened the door.
This time she bought a poison comb,
a curved eight-inch scorpion,
and put it in her hair and swooned again.
The dwarfs returned and took out the comb
and she revived miraculously.
She opened her eyes as wide as Orphan Annie.
Beware, beware, they said,
but the mirror told,
the queen came,
Snow White, the dumb bunny,
opened the door
and she bit into a poison apple
and fell down for the final time.
When the dwarfs returned
they undid her bodice,
they looked for a comb,
but it did no good.
Though they washed her with wine
and rubbed her with butter
it was to no avail.
She lay as still as a gold piece.

The seven dwarfs could not bring themselves
to bury her in the black ground
so they made a glass coffin
and set it upon the seventh mountain
so that all who passed by
could peek in upon her beauty.
A prince came one June day
and would not budge.
He stayed so long his hair turned green
and still he would not leave.
The dwarfs took pity upon him
and gave him the glass Snow White —
its doll's eyes shut forever —
to keep in his far-off castle.

As the prince's men carried the coffin
they stumbled and dropped it
and the chunk of apple flew out
of her throat and she woke up miraculously.

And thus Snow White became the prince's bride.
The wicked queen was invited to the wedding feast
and when she arrived there were
red-hot iron shoes,
in the manner of red-hot roller skates,
clamped upon her feet.
First your toes will smoke
and then your heels will turn black
and you will fry upward like a frog,
she was told.
And so she danced until she was dead,
a subterranean figure,
her tongue flicking in and out
like a gas jet.
Meanwhile Snow White held court,
rolling her china-blue doll eyes open and shut
and sometimes referring to her mirror
as women do.

Rapunzel

A woman
who loves a woman
is forever young.
The mentor
and the student
feed off each other.
Many a girl
had an old aunt
who locked her in the study
to keep the boys away.
They would play rummy
or lie on the couch
and touch and touch.
Old breast against young breast . . .

Let your dress fall down your shoulder,
come touch a copy of you
for I am at the mercy of rain,
for I have left the three Christs of Ypsilanti,
for I have left the long naps of Ann Arbor
and the church spires have turned to stumps.
The sea bangs into my cloister
for the young politicians are dying,
are dying so hold me, my young dear,
hold me . . .

The yellow rose will turn to cinder
and New York City will fall in
before we are done so hold me,
my young dear, hold me.
Put your pale arms around my neck.
Let me hold your heart like a flower
lest it bloom and collapse.
Give me your skin
as sheer as a cobweb,

let me open it up
and listen in and scoop out the dark.
Give me your nether lips
all puffy with their art
and I will give you angel fire in return.
We are two clouds
glistening in the bottle glass.
We are two birds
washing in the same mirror.
We were fair game
but we have kept out of the cesspool.
We are strong.
We are the good ones.
Do not discover us
for we lie together all in green
like pond weeds.
Hold me, my young dear, hold me.

They touch their delicate watches
one at a time.
They dance to the lute
two at a time.
They are as tender as bog moss.
They play mother-me-do
all day.
A woman
who loves a woman
is forever young.

Once there was a witch's garden
more beautiful than Eve's
with carrots growing like little fish,
with many tomatoes rich as frogs,
onions as ingrown as hearts,
the squash singing like a dolphin
and one patch given over wholly to magic —
rampion, a kind of salad root,
a kind of harebell more potent than penicillin,
growing leaf by leaf, skin by skin,

as rapt and as fluid as Isadora Duncan.
However the witch's garden was kept locked
and each day a woman who was with child
looked upon the rampion wildly,
fancying that she would die
if she could not have it.
Her husband feared for her welfare
and thus climbed into the garden
to fetch the life-giving tubers.

Ah ha, cried the witch,
whose proper name was Mother Gothel,
you are a thief and now you will die.
However they made a trade,
typical enough in those times.
He promised his child to Mother Gothel
so of course when it was born
she took the child away with her.
She gave the child the name Rapunzel,
another name for the life-giving rampion.
Because Rapunzel was a beautiful girl
Mother Gothel treasured her beyond all things.
As she grew older Mother Gothel thought:
None but I will ever see her or touch her.
She locked her in a tower without a door
or a staircase. It had only a high window.
When the witch wanted to enter she cried:
Rapunzel, Rapunzel, let down your hair.
Rapunzel's hair fell to the ground like a rainbow.
It was as yellow as a dandelion
and as strong as a dog leash.
Hand over hand she shinnied up
the hair like a sailor
and there in the stone-cold room,
as cold as a museum,
Mother Gothel cried:
Hold me, my young dear, hold me,
and thus they played mother-me-do.

Years later a prince came by
and heard Rapunzel singing in her loneliness.
That song pierced his heart like a valentine
but he could find no way to get to her.
Like a chameleon he hid himself among the trees
and watched the witch ascend the swinging hair.
The next day he himself called out:
Rapunzel, Rapunzel, let down your hair,
and thus they met and he declared his love.
What is this beast, she thought,
with muscles on his arms
like a bag of snakes?
What is this moss on his legs?
What prickly plant grows on his cheeks?
What is this voice as deep as a dog?
Yet he dazzled her with his answers.
Yet he dazzled her with his dancing stick.
They lay together upon the yellowy threads,
swimming through them
like minnows through kelp
and they sang out benedictions like the Pope.

Each day he brought her a skein of silk
to fashion a ladder so they could both escape.
But Mother Gothel discovered the plot
and cut off Rapunzel's hair to her ears
and took her into the forest to repent.
When the prince came the witch fastened
the hair to a hook and let it down.
When he saw that Rapunzel had been banished
he flung himself out of the tower, a side of beef.
He was blinded by thorns that pricked him like tacks.
As blind as Oedipus he wandered for years
until he heard a song that pierced his heart
like that long-ago valentine.
As he kissed Rapunzel her tears fell on his eyes
and in the manner of such cure-alls
his sight was suddenly restored.

They lived happily as you might expect
proving that mother-me-do
can be outgrown,
just as the fish on Friday,
just as a tricycle.
The world, some say,
is made up of couples.
A rose must have a stem.

As for Mother Gothel,
her heart shrank to the size of a pin,
never again to say: Hold me, my young dear,
hold me,
and only as she dreamt of the yellow hair
did moonlight sift into her mouth.

One-Eye, Two-Eyes, Three-Eyes

Even in the pink crib
the somehow deficient,
the somehow maimed,
are thought to have
a special pipeline to the mystical,
the faint smell of the occult,
a large ear on the God-horn.

Still,
the parents have bizarre thoughts,
thoughts like a skill saw.
They accuse: Your grandfather,
your bad sperm, your evil ovary.
Thinking: The devil has put his finger upon us.
And yet in time
they consult their astrologer
and admire their trophy.
They turn a radish into a ruby.
They plan an elaborate celebration.
They warm to their roles.
They carry it off with a positive fervor.
The bird who cannot fly
is left like a cockroach.
A three-legged kitten is carried
by the scruff of the neck
and dropped into a blind cellar hole.
A malformed foal would not be nursed.
Nature takes care of nature.

I knew a child once
With the mind of a hen.
She was the favored one
for she was as innocent as a snowflake
and was a great lover of music.
She could have been a candidate

for the International Bach Society
but she was only a primitive.
A harmonica would do.

Love grew around her like crabgrass.
Even though she might live to the age of fifty
her mother planned a Mass of the Angels
and wore her martyrdom
like a string of pearls.

The unusual needs to be commented upon . . .
The Thalidomide babies
with flippers at their shoulders,
wearing their mechanical arms
like derricks.
The club-footed boy
wearing his shoe like a flat iron.
The idiot child,
a stuffed doll who can only masturbate.
The hunchback carrying his hump
like a bag of onions . . .
Oh how we treasure
their scenic value.

When a child stays needy until he is fifty —
oh mother-eye, oh mother-eye, crush me in —
the parent is as strong as a telephone pole.

Once upon a time
there were three sisters.
One with one eye
like a great blue aggie.
One with two eyes,
common as pennies.
One with three eyes,
the third like an intern.
Their mother loved only One-Eye and Three.
She loved them because they were God's lie.

And she liked to poke
at the unusual holes in their faces.
Two-Eyes was as ordinary
as an old man with a big belly
and she despised her.
Two-Eyes wore only rags
and ate only scraps from the dog's dish
and spent her days caring for their goat.

One day,
off in the fields with the goat,
Two-Eyes cried, her cheeks as wet as a trout
and an old woman appeared before her
and promised if she sang to her goat
a feast would always be provided.
Two-Eyes sang and there appeared a table
as rich as one at Le Pavillon
and each dish bloomed like floribunda.
Two-Eyes, her eyes as matched as a pen and pencil set,
ate all she could.
This went on in a secret manner
until the mother and sisters saw
that she was not lapping from the dog dish.
So One-Eye came with her and her goat
to see where and how she got the secret food.
However Two-Eyes sang to her as softly as milk
and soon she fell fast asleep.
In this way Two-Eyes enjoyed her usual magic meal.
Next the mother sent Three-Eyes to watch.
Again Two-Eyes sang and again her sister fell asleep.
However her third eye did not shut.
It stayed as open as a clam on a half shell
and thus she witnessed the magic meal,
thus the mother heard all of it
and thus they killed the goat.

Again Two-Eyes cried like a trout
and again the old woman came to her
and told her to take some of the insides
of the slaughtered goat and bury them
in front of the cottage.
She carried forth the green and glossy intestine
and buried it where she was told.
The next morning they all saw
a great tree with leaves of silver
glittering like tinfoil
and apples made of fourteen carat gold.
One-Eye tried to climb up and pick one
but the branches merely withdrew.
Three-Eyes tried and the branches withdrew.
The mother tried and the branches withdrew.
May I try, said Two-Eyes,
but they replied:
You with your two eyes,
what can you do?
Yet when she climbed up and reached out
an apple came into her hand
as simply as a chicken laying her daily egg.

They bade her come down from the tree to hide
as a handsome knight was riding their way.
He stopped
and admired the tree
as you knew he would.
They claimed the tree as theirs
and he said sadly:
He who owns a branch of that tree
would have all he wished for in this world.
The two sisters clipped around the tree
like a pair of miming clowns
but not a branch or an apple came their way.
The tree treated them like poison ivy.
At last Two-Eyes came forth
and easily broke off a branch for him.

Quite naturally the knight carried her off
and the sisters were overjoyed
as now the tree would belong to them.
It burned in their brains like radium
but the next morning the tree had vanished.
The tree had, in the way of such magic,
followed Two-Eyes to the castle.
The knight married her
and she wore gowns as lovely as kisses
and ate goose liver and peaches
whenever she wished.

Years later
two beggars came to the castle,
along with the fishermen and the peasants
and the whole mournful lot.
These beggars were none other than her sisters
wearing their special eyes,
one the Cyclops,
one the pawnshop.
Two-Eyes was kind to them
and took them in
for they were magical.
They were to become her Stonehenge,
her cosmic investment,
her seals, her rings, her urns
and she became as strong as Moses.
Two-Eyes was kind to them
and took them in
because they were needy.
They were to become her children,
her charmed cripples, her hybrids —
oh mother-eye, oh mother-eye, crush me in.
So they took root in her heart
with their religious hunger.

The Frog Prince

Frau Doktor,
Mama Brundig,
take out your contacts,
remove your wig.

I write for you.
I entertain.
But frogs come out
of the sky like rain.

Frogs arrive
With an ugly fury.
You are my judge.
You are my jury.

My guilts are what
we catalogue.
I'll take a knife
and chop up frog.

Frog has no nerves.
Frog is as old as a cockroach.
Frog is my father's genitals.
Frog is a malformed doorknob.
Frog is a soft bag of green.

The moon will not have him.
The sun wants to shut off
like a light bulb.
At the sight of him
the stone washes itself in a tub.
The crow thinks he's an apple
and drops a worm in.
At the feel of frog
the touch-me-nots explode
like electric slugs.

Slime will have him.
Slime has made him a house.

Mr. Poison
is at my bed.
He wants my sausage.
He wants my bread.

Mama Brundig,
he wants my beer.
He wants my Christ
for a souvenir.

Frog has boil disease
and a bellyful of parasites.
He says: Kiss me. Kiss me.
And the ground soils itself.

Why
should a certain
quite adorable princess
be walking in her garden
at such a time
and toss her golden ball
up like a bubble
and drop it into the well?
It was ordained.
Just as the fates deal out
the plague with a tarot card.
Just as the Supreme Being drills
holes in our skulls to let
the Boston Symphony through.

But I digress.
A loss has taken place.
The ball has sunk like a cast-iron pot
into the bottom of the well.

Lost, she said,
my moon, my butter calf,
my yellow moth, my Hindu hare.
Obviously it was more than a ball.
Balls such as these are not
for sale in Au Bon Marché.
I took the moon, she said,
between my teeth
and now it is gone
and I am lost forever.
A thief had robbed by day.

Suddenly the well grew
thick and boiling
and a frog appeared.
His eyes bulged like two peas
and his body was trussed into place.
Do not be afraid, Princess,
he said, I am not a vagabond,
a cattle farmer, a shepherd,
a doorkeeper, a postman
or a laborer.
I come to you as a tradesman.
I have something to sell.
Your ball, he said,
for just three things.
Let me eat from your plate.
Let me drink from your cup.
Let me sleep in your bed.
She thought, Old Waddler,
those three you will never do,
but she made the promises
with hopes for her ball once more.
He brought it up in his mouth
like a tricky old dog
and she ran back to the castle
leaving the frog quite alone.

That evening at dinner time
a knock was heard at the castle door
and a voice demanded:
King's youngest daughter,
let me in. You promised;
now open to me.
I have left the skunk cabbage
and the eels to live with you.
The king then heard of her promise
and forced her to comply.

The frog first sat on her lap.
He was as awful as an undertaker.
Next he was at her plate
looking over her bacon
and calves' liver.
We will eat in tandem,
he said gleefully.
Her fork trembled
as if a small machine
had entered her.
He sat upon the liver
and partook like a gourmet.
The princess choked
as if she were eating a puppy.
From her cup he drank.
It wasn't exactly hygienic.
From her cup she drank
as if it were Socrates' hemlock.

Next came the bed.
The silky royal bed.
Ah! The penultimate hour!
There was the pillow
with the princess breathing
and there was the sinuous frog
riding up and down beside her.
I have been lost in a river
of shut doors, he said,

and I have made my way over
the wet stones to live with you.
She woke up aghast.
I suffer for birds and fireflies
but not frogs, she said,
and threw him across the room.
Kaboom!

Like a genie coming out of a samovar,
a handsome prince arose in the
corner of her royal bedroom.
He had kind eyes and hands
and was a friend of sorrow.
Thus they were married.
After all he had compromised her.

He hired a night watchman
so that no one could enter the chamber
and he had the well
boarded over so that
never again would she lose her ball,
that moon, that Krishna hair,
that blind poppy, that innocent globe,
that madonna womb.

Briar Rose (Sleeping Beauty)

Consider
a girl who keeps slipping off,
arms limp as old carrots,
into the hypnotist's trance,
into a spirit world
speaking with the gift of tongues.
She is stuck in the time machine,
suddenly two years old sucking her thumb,
as inward as a snail,
learning to talk again.
She's on a voyage.
She is swimming further and further back,
up like a salmon,
struggling into her mother's pocketbook.
Little doll child,
come here to Papa.
Sit on my knee.
I have kisses for the back of your neck.
A penny for your thoughts, Princess.
I will hunt them like an emerald.
Come be my snooky
and I will give you a root.
That kind of voyage,
rank as honeysuckle.

Once
a king had a christening
for his daughter Briar Rose
and because he had only twelve gold plates
he asked only twelve fairies
to the grand event.
The thirteenth fairy,
her fingers as long and thin as straws,
her eyes burnt by cigarettes,
her uterus an empty teacup,

arrived with an evil gift.
She made this prophecy:
The princess shall prick herself
on a spinning wheel in her fifteenth year
and then fall down dead.
Kaputt!
The court fell silent.
The king looked like Munch's *Scream.*
Fairies' prophecies,
in times like those,
held water.
However the twelfth fairy
had a certain kind of eraser
and thus she mitigated the curse
changing that death
into a hundred-year sleep.

The king ordered every spinning wheel
exterminated and exorcized.
Briar Rose grew to be a goddess
and each night the king
bit the hem of her gown
to keep her safe.
He fastened the moon up
with a safety pin
to give her perpetual light
He forced every male in the court
to scour his tongue with Bab-o
lest they poison the air she dwelt in.
Thus she dwelt in his odor.
Rank as honeysuckle.

On her fifteenth birthday
she pricked her finger
on a charred spinning wheel
and the clocks stopped.
Yes indeed. She went to sleep.
The king and queen went to sleep,
the courtiers, the flies on the wall.

The fire in the hearth grew still
and the roast meat stopped crackling.
The trees turned into metal
and the dog became china.
They all lay in a trance,
each a catatonic
stuck in the time machine.
Even the frogs were zombies.
Only a bunch of briar roses grew
forming a great wall of tacks
around the castle.
Many princes
tried to get through the brambles
for they had heard much of Briar Rose
but they had not scoured their tongues
so they were held by the thorns
and thus were crucified.
In due time
a hundred years passed
and a prince got through.
The briars parted as if for Moses
and the prince found the tableau intact.
He kissed Briar Rose
and she woke up crying:
Daddy! Daddy!
Presto! She's out of prison!
She married the prince
and all went well
except for the fear —
the fear of sleep.

Briar Rose
was an insomniac . . .
She could not nap
or lie in sleep
without the court chemist
mixing her some knock-out drops
and never in the prince's presence.
If it is to come, she said,

sleep must take me unawares
while I am laughing or dancing
so that I do not know that brutal place
where I lie down with cattle prods,
the hole in my cheek open.
Further, I must not dream
for when I do I see the table set
and a faltering crone at my place,
her eyes burnt by cigarettes
as she eats betrayal like a slice of meat.

I must not sleep
for while asleep I'm ninety
and think I'm dying.
Death rattles in my throat
like a marble.
I wear tubes like earrings.
I lie as still as a bar of iron.
You can stick a needle
through my kneecap and I won't flinch.
I'm all shot up with Novocain.
This trance girl
is yours to do with.
You could lay her in a grave,
an awful package,
and shovel dirt on her face
and she'd never call back: Hello there!
But if you kissed her on the mouth
her eyes would spring open
and she'd call out: Daddy! Daddy!
Presto!
She's out of prison.

There was a theft.
That much I am told.
I was abandoned.
That much I know.
I was forced backward.
I was forced forward.

I was passed hand to hand
like a bowl of fruit.
Each night I am nailed into place
and I forget who I am.
Daddy?
That's another kind of prison.
It's not the prince at all,
but my father
drunkenly bent over my bed,
circling the abyss like a shark,
my father thick upon me
like some sleeping jellyfish.
What voyage this, little girl?
This coming out of prison?
God help —
this life after death?

From The Book of Folly

(1972)

Mother and Daughter

Linda, you are leaving
your old body now.
It lies flat, an old butterfly,
all arm, all leg, all wing,
loose as an old dress.
I reach out toward it but
my fingers turn to cankers
and I am motherwarm and used,
just as your childhood is used.
Question you about this
and you hold up pearls.
Question you about this
and you pass by armies.
Question you about this —
you with your big clock going,
its hands wider than jackstraws —
and you'll sew up a continent.

Now that you are eighteen
I give you my booty, my spoils,
my Mother & Co. and my ailments.
Question you about this
and you'll not know the answer —
the muzzle at the mouth,
the hopeful tent of oxygen,
the tubes, the pathways,
the war and the war's vomit.
Keep on, keep on, keep on,
carrying keepsakes to the boys,
carrying powders to the boys,
carrying, my Linda, blood to
the bloodletter.

Linda, you are leaving
your old body now.
You've picked my pocket clean
and you've racked up all my
poker chips and left me empty
and, as the river between us
narrows, you do calisthenics,
that womanly leggy semaphore.
Question you about this
and you will sew me a shroud
and hold up Monday's broiler
and thumb out the chicken gut.
Question you about this
and you will see my death
drooling at these gray lips
while you, my burglar, will eat
fruit and pass the time of day.

Dreaming the Breasts

Mother,
strange goddess face
above my milk home,
that delicate asylum,
I ate you up.
All my need took
you down like a meal.

What you gave
I remember in a dream:
the freckled arms binding me,
the laugh somewhere over my woolly hat,
the blood fingers tying my shoe,
the breasts hanging like two bats
and then darting at me,
bending me down.

The breasts I knew at midnight
beat like the sea in me now.
Mother, I put bees in my mouth
to keep from eating
yet it did you no good.
In the end they cut off your breasts
and milk poured from them
into the surgeon's hand
and he embraced them.
I took them from him
and planted them.

I have put a padlock
on you, Mother, dear dead human,
so that your great bells,
those dear white ponies,
can go galloping, galloping,
wherever you are.

The Silence

The more I write, the more the silence seems
to be eating away at me.

— C. K. Williams

My room is whitewashed,
as white as a rural station house
and just as silent;
whiter than chicken bones
bleaching in the moonlight,
pure garbage,
and just as silent.
There is a white statue behind me
and white plants
growing like obscene virgins,
pushing out their rubbery tongues
but saying nothing.

My hair is the one dark.
It has been burnt in the white fire
and is just a char.
My beads too are black,
twenty eyes heaved up
from the volcano,
quite contorted.

I am filling the room
with the words from my pen.
Words leak out of it like a miscarriage.
I am zinging words out into the air
and they come back like squash balls.
Yet there is silence.
Always silence.
Like an enormous baby mouth.

The silence is death.
It comes each day with its shock
to sit on my shoulder, a white bird,
and peck at the black eyes
and the vibrating red muscle
of my mouth.

From The Death of the Fathers

I. OYSTERS

Oysters we ate,
sweet blue babies,
twelve eyes looked up at me,
running with lemon and Tabasco.
I was afraid to eat this father-food
and Father laughed
and drank down his martini,
clear as tears.
It was a soft medicine
that came from the sea into my mouth,
moist and plump.
I swallowed.
It went down like a large pudding.
Then I ate one o'clock and two o'clock.
Then I laughed and then we laughed
and let me take note —
there was a death,
the death of childhood
there at the Union Oyster House
for I was fifteen
and eating oysters
and the child was defeated.
The woman won.

2. HOW WE DANCED

The night of my cousin's wedding
I wore blue.
I was nineteen
and we danced, Father, we orbited.
We moved like angels washing themselves.
We moved like two birds on fire.

Then we moved like the sea in a jar,
slower and slower.
The orchestra played
"Oh how we danced on the night we were wed."
And you waltzed me like a lazy Susan
and we were dear,
very dear.
Now that you are laid out,
useless as a blind dog,
now that you no longer lurk,
the song rings in my head.
Pure oxygen was the champagne we drank
and clicked our glasses, one to one.
The champagne breathed like a skin diver
and the glasses were crystal and the bride
and groom gripped each other in sleep
like nineteen-thirty marathon dancers.
Mother was a belle and danced with twenty men.
You danced with me never saying a word.
Instead the serpent spoke as you held me close.
The serpent, that mocker, woke up and pressed against me
like a great god and we bent together
like two lonely swans.

3. THE BOAT

Father
(he calls himself
"old sea dog"),
in his yachting cap
at the wheel of the Chris-Craft,
a mahogany speedboat
named *Go Too III,*
speeds out past Cuckold's Light
over the dark brainy blue.
I in the very back
with an orange life jacket on.
I in the dare seat.

Mother up front.
Her kerchief flapping.
The waves deep as whales.
(Whales in fact have been sighted.
A school two miles out of Boothbay Harbor.)
It is bumpy and we are going too fast.
The waves are boulders that we ride upon.
I am seven and we are riding
to Pemaquid or Spain.
Now the waves are higher;
they are round buildings.
We start to go through them
and the boat shudders.
Father is going faster.
I am wet.
I am tumbling on my seat
like a loose kumquat.
Suddenly
a wave that we go under.
Under. Under. Under.
We are daring the sea.
We have parted it.
We are scissors.
Here in the green room
the dead are very close.
Here in the pitiless green
where there are no keepsakes
or cathedrals an angel spoke:
You have no business.
No business here.
Give me a sign,
cries Father,
and the sky breaks over us.
There is air to have.
There are gulls kissing the boat.
There is the sun as big as a nose.
And here are the three of us
dividing our deaths,
bailing the boat

and closing out
the cold wing that has clasped us
this bright August day.

4. SANTA

Father,
the Santa Claus suit
you bought from Wolff Fording Theatrical Supplies,
back before I was born,
is dead.
The white beard you fooled me with
and the hair like Moses,
the thick crimpy wool
that used to buzz me on the neck,
is dead.
Yes, my busting rosy Santa,
ringing your bronze cowbell.
You with real soot on your nose
and snow (taken from the refrigerator some years)
on your big shoulder.
The room was like Florida.
You took so many oranges out of your bag
and threw them around the living room,
all the time laughing that North Pole laugh.
Mother would kiss you
for she was that tall.
Mother could hug you
for she was not afraid.
The reindeer pounded on the roof.
(It was my Nana with a hammer in the attic.
For *my* children it was my husband
with a crowbar breaking things up.)
The year I ceased to believe in you
is the year you were drunk.
My boozy red man,
your voice all slithery like soap,

you were a long way from Saint Nick
with Daddy's cocktail smell.
I cried and ran from the room
and you said, "Well, thank God that's over!"
And it was, until the grandchildren came.
Then I tied up your pillows
in the five A.M. Christ morning
and I adjusted the beard,
all yellow with age,
and applied rouge to your cheeks
and Chalk White to your eyebrows.
We were conspirators,
secret actors,
and I kissed you
because I was tall enough.
But that is over.
The era closes
and large children hang their stockings
and build a black memorial to you.
And you, you fade out of sight
like a lost signalman
wagging his lantern
for the train that comes no more.

Angels of the Love Affair

"Angels of the love affair, do you know that other,
the dark one, that other me?"

1. ANGEL OF FIRE AND GENITALS

Angel of fire and genitals, do you know slime,
that green mama who first forced me to sing,
who put me first in the latrine, that pantomime
of brown where I was beggar and she was king?
I said, "The devil is down that festering hole."
Then he bit me in the buttocks and took over my soul.
Fire woman, you of the ancient flame, you
of the Bunsen burner, you of the candle,
you of the blast furnace, you of the barbecue,
you of the fierce solar energy, Mademoiselle,
take some ice, take some snow, take a month of rain
and you would gutter in the dark, cracking up your brain.

Mother of fire, let me stand at your devouring gate
as the sun dies in your arms and you loosen its terrible
    weight.

2. ANGEL OF CLEAN SHEETS

Angel of clean sheets, do you know bedbugs?
Once in a madhouse they came like specks of cinnamon
as I lay in a chloral cave of drugs,
as old as a dog, as quiet as a skeleton.
Little bits of dried blood. One hundred marks
upon the sheet. One hundred kisses in the dark.
White sheets smelling of soap and Clorox
have nothing to do with this night of soil,

nothing to do with barred windows and multiple locks
and all the webbing in the bed, the ultimate recoil.
I have slept in silk and in red and in black.
I have slept on sand and, one fall night, a haystack.

I have known a crib. I have known the tuck-in of a child
but inside my hair waits the night I was defiled.

3. ANGEL OF FLIGHT AND SLEIGH BELLS

Angel of flight and sleigh bells, do you know paralysis,
that ether house where your arms and legs are cement?
You are as still as a yardstick. You have a doll's kiss.
The brain whirls in a fit. The brain is not evident.
I have gone to that same place without a germ or a stroke.
A little solo act — that lady with the brain that broke.

In this fashion I have become a tree.
I have become a vase you can pick up or drop at will,
inanimate at last. What unusual luck! My body
passively resisting. Part of the leftovers. Part of the kill.
Angel of flight, you soarer, you flapper, you floater,
you gull that grows out of my back in the dreams I prefer,

stay near. But give me the totem. Give me the shut eye
where I stand in stone shoes as the world's bicycle goes by.

4. ANGEL OF HOPE AND CALENDARS

Angel of hope and calendars, do you know despair?
That hole I crawl into with a box of Kleenex,
that hole where the fire woman is tied to her chair,
that hole where leather men are wringing their necks,
where the sea has turned into a pond of urine.
There is no place to wash and no marine beings to stir in.

In this hole your mother is crying out each day.
Your father is eating cake and digging her grave.
In this hole your baby is strangling. Your mouth is clay.
Your eyes are made of glass. They break. You are not brave.
You are alone like a dog in a kennel. Your hands
break out in boils. Your arms are cut and bound by bands

of wire. Your voice is out there. Your voice is strange.
There are no prayers here. Here there is no change.

5. ANGEL OF BLIZZARDS AND BLACKOUTS

Angel of blizzards and blackouts, do you know raspberries,
those rubies that sat in the green of my grandfather's garden?
You of the snow tires, you of the sugary wings, you freeze
me out. Let me crawl through the patch. Let me be ten.
Let me pick those sweet kisses, thief that I was,
as the sea on my left slapped its applause.

Only my grandfather was allowed there. Or the maid
who came with a scullery pan to pick for breakfast.
She of the rolls that floated in the air, she of the inlaid
woodwork all greasy with lemon, she of the feather and
    dust,
not I. Nonetheless I came sneaking across the salt lawn
in bare feet and jumping-jack pajamas in the spongy dawn.

Oh Angel of the blizzard and blackout, Madam white face,
take me back to that red mouth, that July 21st place.

6. ANGEL OF BEACH HOUSES AND PICNICS

Angel of beach houses and picnics, do you know solitaire?
Fifty-two reds and blacks and only myself to blame.
My blood buzzes like a hornet's nest. I sit in a kitchen chair
at a table set for one. The silverware is the same

and the glass and the sugar bowl. I hear my lungs fill and expel
as in an operation. But I have no one left to tell.

Once I was a couple. I was my own king and queen
with cheese and bread and rosé on the rocks of Rockport.
Once I sunbathed in the buff, all brown and lean,
watching the toy sloops go by, holding court
for busloads of tourists. Once I called breakfast the sexiest
meal of the day. Once I invited arrest

at the peace march in Washington. Once I was young and bold
and left hundreds of unmatched people out in the cold.

Jesus Suckles

Mary, your great
white apples make me glad.
I feel your heart work its
machine and I doze like a fly.
I cough like a bird on its worm.
I'm a jelly-baby and you're my wife.
You're a rock and I the fringy algae.
You're a lily and I'm the bee that gets inside.
I close my eyes and suck you in like a fire.
I grow. I grow. I'm fattening out.
I'm a kid in a rowboat and you're the sea,
the salt, you're every fish of importance.

No. No.
All lies.
I am small
and you hold me.
You give me milk
and we are the same
and I am glad.

No. No.
All lies.
I am a truck. I run everything.
I own you.

Jesus Awake

It was the year
of the How To Sex Book,
the Sensuous Man and Woman were frolicking
but Jesus was fasting.
He ate His celibate life.
the ground shuddered like an ocean,
a great sexual swell under His feet.
His scrolls bit each other.
He was shrouded in gold like nausea.
Outdoors the kitties hung from their mother's tits
like sausages in a smokehouse.
Roosters cried all day, hammering for love.
Blood flowed from the kitchen pump
but He was fasting.
His sex was sewn onto Him like a medal
and His penis no longer arched with sorrow over Him.
He was fasting.
He was like a great house
with no people,
no plans.

Jesus Asleep

Jesus slept as still as a toy
and in His dream
He desired Mary.
His penis sang like a dog,
but He turned sharply away from that play
like a door slamming.
That door broke His heart
for He had a sore need.
He made a statue out of His need.
With His penis like a chisel
He carved the Pietà.
At this death it was important to have only one desire.
He carved this death.
He was persistent.
He died over and over again.
He swam up and up a pipe toward it,
breathing water through His gills.
He swam through stone.
He swam through the godhead
and because He had not known Mary
they were united at His death,
the cross to the woman,
in a final embrace,
poised forever
like a centerpiece.

Jesus Raises Up the Harlot

The harlot squatted
with her hands over her red hair.
She was not looking for customers.
She was in a deep fear.
A delicate body clothed in red,
as red as a smashed fist
and she was bloody as well
for the townspeople were trying
to stone her to death.
Stones came at her like bees to candy
and sweet redheaded harlot that she was
she screamed out, *I never, I never.*
Rocks flew out of her mouth like pigeons
and Jesus saw this and thought to
exhume her like a mortician.

Jesus knew that a terrible sickness
dwelt in the harlot and He could lance it
with His two small thumbs.
He held up His hand and the stones
dropped to the ground like doughnuts.
Again He held up His hand
and the harlot came and kissed Him.
He lanced her twice. On the spot.
He lanced her twice on each breast,
pushing His thumbs in until the milk ran out,
those two boils of whoredom.
The harlot followed Jesus around like a puppy
for He had raised her up.
Now she forsook her fornications
and became His pet.
His raising her up made her feel
like a little girl again when she had a father
who brushed the dirt from her eye.
Indeed, she took hold of herself,
knowing she owed Jesus a life,
as sure-fire as a trump card.

Jesus Cooks

Jesus saw the multitudes were hungry
and He said, Oh Lord,
send down a short-order cook.
And the Lord said, Abracadabra.
Jesus took the fish,
a slim green baby,
in His right hand and said, Oh Lord,
and the Lord said,
Work on the sly
opening boxes of sardine cans.
And He did.
Fisherman, fisherman,
you make it look easy.
And lo, there were many fish.
Next Jesus held up a loaf
and said, Oh Lord,
and the Lord instructed Him
like an assembly-line baker man,
a Pied Piper of yeast,
and lo, there were many.

Jesus passed among the people
in a chef's hat
and they kissed His spoons and forks
and ate well from invisible dishes.

Jesus Summons Forth

Jesus saw Lazarus.
Lazarus was likely in heaven,
as dead as a pear
and the very same light green color.
Jesus thought to summon him
forth from his grave.
Oh hooded one, He cried,
come unto Me.
Lazarus smiled the smile of the dead
like a fool sucking on a dry stone.
Oh hooded one,
cried Jesus,
and it did no good.
The Lord spoke to Jesus
and gave Him instructions.
First Jesus put on the wrists,
then He inserted the hip bone,
He tapped in the vertebral column,
He fastened the skull down.
Lazarus was whole.
Jesus put His mouth to Lazarus's
and a current shot between them for a moment.
Then came tenderness.
Jesus rubbed all the flesh of Lazarus
and at last the heart, poor old wound,
started up in spite of itself.
Lazarus opened one eye. It was watchful.
And then Jesus picked him up
and set him upon his two sad feet.

His soul dropped down from heaven.
Thank you, said Lazarus,
for in heaven it had been no different.
In heaven there had been no change.

Jesus Dies

From up here in the crow's nest
I see a small crowd gather.
Who do you gather, my townsmen?
There is no news here.
I am not a trapeze artist.
I am busy with My dying.
Three heads lolling,
bobbing like bladders.
No news.
The soldiers down below
laughing as soldiers have done for centuries.
No news.
We are the same men,
you and I,
the same sort of nostrils,
the same sort of feet.
My bones are oiled with blood
and so are yours.
My heart pumps like a jack rabbit in a trap
and so does yours.
I want to kiss God on His nose and watch Him sneeze
and so do you.
Not out of disrespect.
Out of pique.
Out of a man-to-man thing.
I want heaven to descend and sit on My dinner plate
and so do you.
I want God to put His steaming arms around Me
and so do you.
Because we need.
Because we are sore creatures.
My townsmen,
go home now.

I will do nothing extraordinary.
I will not divide in two.
I will not pick out My white eyes.
Go now,
this is a personal matter,
a private affair and God knows
none of your business.

Jesus Unborn

The gallowstree drops
one hundred heads upon the ground
and in Judea Jesus is unborn.
Mary is not yet with child.
Mary sits in a grove of olive trees
with the small pulse in her neck
beating. Beating the drumbeat.
The well that she dipped her pitcher into
has made her as instinctive as an animal.
Now she would like to lower herself down
like a camel and settle into the soil.
Although she is at the penultimate moment
she would like to doze fitfully like a dog.
She would like to be flattened out like the sea
when it lies down, a field of moles.
Instead a strange being leans over her
and lifts her chin firmly
and gazes at her with executioner's eyes.
Nine clocks spring open
and smash themselves against the sun.
The calendars of the world
burn if you touch them.
All this will be remembered.
Now we will have a Christ.
He covers her like a heavy door
and shuts her lifetime up
into this dump-faced day.

The Author of the Jesus Papers
Speaks

In my dream
I milked a cow,
the terrible udder
like a great rubber lily
sweated in my fingers
and as I yanked,
waiting for the moon juice,
waiting for the white mother,
blood spurted from it
and covered me with shame.
Then God spoke to me and said:
People say only good things about Christmas.
If they want to say something bad,
they whisper.
So I went to the well and drew a baby
out of the hollow water.
Then God spoke to me and said:
Here. Take this gingerbread lady
and put her in your oven.
When the cow gives blood
and the Christ is born
we must all eat sacrifices.
We must all eat beautiful women.

From The Death Notebooks

(1974)

For Mr. Death Who Stands with
   His Door Open

Time grows dim. Time that was so long
grows short, time, all goggle-eyed,
wiggling her skirts, singing her torch song,
giving the boys a buzz and a ride,
that Nazi Mama with her beer and sauerkraut.
Time, old gal of mine, will soon dim out.

May I say how young she was back then,
playing piggley-witch and hoola-hoop,
dancing the jango with six awful men,
letting the chickens out of the coop,
promising to marry Jack and Jerome,
and never bothering, never, never,
to come back home.

Time was when time had time enough
and the sea washed me daily in its delicate brine.
There is no terror when you swim in the buff
or speed up the boat and hang out a line.
Time was when I could hiccup and hold my breath
and not in that instant meet Mr. Death.

Mr. Death, you actor, you have many masks.
Once you were sleek, a kind of Valentino
with my father's bathtub gin in your flask.
With my cinched-in waist and my dumb vertigo
at the crook of your long white arm
and yet you never bent me back, never, never,
into your blackguard charm.

Next, Mr. Death, you held out the bait
during my first decline, as they say,

telling that suicide baby to celebrate
her own going in her own puppet play.
I went out popping pills and crying adieu
in my own death camp with my own little Jew.

Now your beer belly hangs out like Fatso.
You are popping your buttons and expelling gas.
How can I lie down with you, my comical beau
when you are so middle-aged and lower-class.
Yet you'll press me down in your envelope;
pressed as neat as a butterfly, forever, forever,
beside Mussolini and the Pope.

Mr. Death, when you came to the ovens it was short
and to the drowning man you were likewise kind,
and the nicest of all to the baby I had to abort
and middling you were to all the crucified combined.
But when it comes to my death let it be slow,
let it be pantomime, this last peep show,
so that I may squat at the edge trying on
my black necessary trousseau.

The Death Baby

I was an ice baby.
I turned to sky blue.
My tears became two glass beads.
My mouth stiffened into a dumb howl.
They say it was a dream
but I remember that hardening.

My sister at six
dreamt nightly of my death:
"The baby turned to ice.
Someone put her in the refrigerator
and she turned as hard as a Popsicle."

I remember the stink of the liverwurst.
How I was put on a platter and laid
between the mayonnaise and the bacon.
The rhythm of the refrigerator
had been disturbed.
The milk bottle hissed like a snake.
The tomatoes vomited up their stomachs.
The caviar turned to lava.
The pimentos kissed like cupids.
I moved like a lobster,
slower and slower.
The air was tiny.
The air would not do.
        *
I was at the dogs' party.
I was their bone.
I had been laid out in their kennel
like a fresh turkey.

This was my sister's dream
but I remember that quartering;
I remember the sickbed smell
of the sawdust floor, the pink eyes,
the pink tongues and the teeth, those nails.
I had been carried out like Moses
and hidden by the paws
of ten Boston bull terriers,
ten angry bulls
jumping like enormous roaches.
At first I was lapped,
rough as sandpaper.
I became very clean.
Then my arm was missing.
I was coming apart.
They loved me until
I was gone.

2. THE DY-DEE DOLL

My Dy-dee doll
died twice.
Once when I snapped
her head off
and let it float in the toilet
and once under the sun lamp
trying to get warm
she melted.
She was a gloom,
her face embracing
her little bent arms.
She died in all her rubber wisdom.

3. SEVEN TIMES

I died seven times
in seven ways
letting death give me a sign,
letting death place his mark on my forehead,
crossed over, crossed over.

And death took root in that sleep.
In that sleep I held an ice baby
and I rocked it
and was rocked by it.
Oh Madonna, hold me.
I am a small handful.

4. MADONNA

My mother died
unrocked, unrocked.
Weeks at her deathbed
seeing her thrust herself against the metal bars,
thrashing like a fish on the hook
and me low at her high stage,
letting the priestess dance alone,
wanting to place my head in her lap
or even take her in my arms somehow
and fondle her twisted gray hair.
But her rocking horse was pain
with vomit steaming from her mouth.
Her belly was big with another child,
cancer's baby, big as a football.
I could not soothe.
With every hump and crack
there was less Madonna
until that strange labor took her.
Then the room was bankrupt.
That was the end of her paying.

5 . MAX

Max and I
two immoderate sisters,
two immoderate writers,
two burdeners,
made a pact.
To beat death down with a stick.
To take over.
To build our death like carpenters.
When she had a broken back,
each night we built her sleep.
Talking on the hot line
until her eyes pulled down like shades.
And we agreed in those long hushed phone calls
that when the moment comes
we'll talk turkey,
we'll shoot words straight from the hip,
we'll play it as it lays.
Yes,
when death comes with its hood
we won't be polite.

6 . BABY

Death,
you lie in my arms like a cherub,
as heavy as bread dough.
Your milky wings are as still as plastic.
Hair as soft as music.
Hair the color of a harp.
And eyes made of glass,
as brittle as crystal.
Each time I rock you
I think you will break.
I rock. I rock.
Glass eye, ice eye,
primordial eye,
lava eye,

pin eye,
break eye,
how you stare back!

Like the gaze of small children
you know all about me.
You have worn my underwear.
You have read my newspaper.
You have seen my father whip me.
You have seen me stroke my father's whip.

I rock. I rock.
We plunge back and forth
comforting each other.
We are stone.
We are carved, a pietà
that swings and swings.
Outside, the world is a chilly army.
Outside, the sea is brought to its knees.
Outside, Pakistan is swallowed in a mouthful.

I rock. I rock.
You are my stone child
with still eyes like marbles.
There is a death baby
for each of us.
We own him.
His smell is our smell.
Beware. Beware.
There is a tenderness.
There is a love
for this dumb traveler
waiting in his pink covers.
Someday,
heavy with cancer or disaster
I will look up at Max
and say: It is time.
Hand me the death baby
and there will be
that final rocking.

From The Furies

THE FURY OF BEAUTIFUL BONES

Sing me a thrush, bone.
Sing me a nest of cup and pestle.
Sing me a sweetbread for an old grandfather.
Sing me a foot and a doorknob, for you are my love.
Oh sing, bone bag man, sing.
Your head is what I remember that August,
you were in love with another woman but
that didn't matter. I was the fury of your
bones, your fingers long and nubby, your
forehead a beacon, bare as marble and I worried
you like an odor because you had not quite forgotten,
bone bag man, garlic in the North End,
the book you dedicated, naked as a fish,
naked as someone drowning into his own mouth.
I wonder, Mr. Bone man, what you're thinking
of your fury now, gone sour as a sinking whale,
crawling up the alphabet on her own bones.
Am I in your ear still singing songs in the rain,
me of the death rattle, me of the magnolias,
me of the sawdust tavern at the city's edge.
Women have lovely bones, arms, neck, thigh
and I admire them also, but your bones
supersede loveliness. They are the tough
ones that get broken and reset. I just can't
answer for you, only for your bones,
round rulers, round nudgers, round poles,
numb nubkins, the sword of sugar.
I feel the skull, Mr. Skeleton, living its
own life in its own skin.

This singing
is a kind of dying,
a kind of birth,
a votive candle.
I have a dream-mother
who sings with her guitar,
nursing the bedroom
with moonlight and beautiful olives.
A flute came too,
joining the five strings,
a God finger over the holes.
I knew a beautiful woman once
who sang with her fingertips
and her eyes were brown
like small birds.
At the cup of her breasts
I drew wine.
At the mound of her legs
I drew figs.
She sang for my thirst,
mysterious songs of God
that would have laid an army down.
It was as if a morning-glory
had bloomed in her throat
and all that blue
and small pollen
ate into my heart
violent and religious.

THE FURY OF COOKS

Herbs, garlic,
cheese, please let me in!
Souffles, salads,
Parker House rolls,
please let me in!
Cook Helen,

why are you so cross,
why is your kitchen verboten?
Couldn't you just teach me
to bake a potato,
that charm,
that young prince?
No! No!
This is my country!
You shout silently.
Couldn't you just show me
the gravy. How you drill it out
of the stomach of that bird?
Helen, Helen,
let me in,
let me feel the flour,
is it blind and frightening,
this stuff that makes cakes?
Helen, Helen,
the kitchen is your dog
and you pat it
and love it
and keep it clean.
But all these things,
all these dishes of things
come through the swinging door
and I don't know from where?
Give me some tomato aspic, Helen!
I don't want to be alone.

THE FURY OF COCKS

There they are
drooping over the breakfast plates,
angel-like,
folding in their sad wing,
animal sad,
and only the night before
there they were
playing the banjo.

Once more the day's light comes
with its immense sun,
its mother trucks,
its engines of amputation.
Whereas last night
the cock knew its way home,
as stiff as a hammer,
battering in with all
its awful power.
That theater.
Today it is tender,
a small bird,
as soft as a baby's hand.
She is the house.
He is the steeple.
When they fuck they are God.
When they break away they are God.
When they snore they are God.
In the morning they butter the toast.
They don't say much.
They are still God.
All the cocks of the world are God,
blooming, blooming, blooming
into the sweet blood of woman.

THE FURY OF SUNSETS

Something
cold is in the air,
an aura of ice
and phlegm.
All day I've built
a lifetime and now
the sun sinks to
undo it.
The horizon bleeds
and sucks its thumb.
The little red thumb
goes out of sight.

And I wonder about
this lifetime with myself,
this dream I'm living.
I could eat the sky
like an apple
but I'd rather
ask the first star:
why am I here?
why do I live in this house?
who's responsible?
eh?

THE FURY OF SUNRISES

Darkness
as black as your eyelid,
poketricks of stars,
the yellow mouth,
the smell of a stranger,
dawn coming up,
dark blue,
no stars,
the smell of a lover,
warmer now
as authentic as soap,
wave after wave
of lightness
and the birds in their chains
going mad with throat noises,
the birds in their tracks
yelling into their cheeks like clowns,
lighter, lighter,
the stars gone,
the trees appearing in their green hoods,
the house appearing across the way,
the road and its sad macadam,
the rock walls losing their cotton,
lighter, lighter,

letting the dog out and seeing
fog lift by her legs,
a gauze dance,
lighter, lighter,
yellow, blue at the tops of trees,
more God, more God everywhere,
lighter, lighter,
more world everywhere,
sheets bent back for people,
the strange heads of love
and breakfast,
that sacrament,
lighter, yellower,
like the yolk of eggs,
the flies gathering at the windowpane,
the dog inside whining for food
and the day commencing,
not to die, not to die,
as in the last day breaking,
a final day digesting itself,
lighter, lighter,
the endless colors,
the same old trees stepping toward me,
the rock unpacking its crevices,
breakfast like a dream
and the whole day to live through,
steadfast, deep, interior.
After the death,
after the black of black,
this lightness —
not to die, not to die —
that God begot.

Clothes

Put on a clean shirt
before you die, some Russian said.
Nothing with drool, please,
no egg spots, no blood,
no sweat, no sperm.
You want me clean, God,
so I'll try to comply.

The hat I was married in,
will it do?
White, broad, fake flowers in a tiny array.
It's old-fashioned, as stylish as a bedbug,
but it suits to die in something nostalgic.

And I'll take
my painting shirt
washed over and over of course
spotted with every yellow kitchen I've painted.
God, you don't mind if I bring all my kitchens?
They hold the family laughter and the soup.

For a bra
(need we mention it?),
the padded black one that my lover demeaned
when I took it off.
He said, "Where'd it all go?"

And I'll take
the maternity skirt of my ninth month,
a window for the love-belly
that let each baby pop out like an apple,
the water breaking in the restaurant,
making a noisy house I'd like to die in.

For underpants I'll pick white cotton,
the briefs of my childhood,
for it was my mother's dictum
that nice girls wore only white cotton.
If my mother had lived to see it
she would have put a WANTED sign up in the post office
for the black, the red, the blue I've worn.
Still, it would be perfectly fine with me
to die like a nice girl
smelling of Clorox and Duz.
Being sixteen-in-the-pants
I would die full of questions.

From O Ye Tongues

Let there be a God as large as a sunlamp to laugh his heat at you.

Let there be an earth with a form like a jigsaw and let it fit for all of ye.

Let there be the darkness of a darkroom out of the deep. A worm room.

Let there be a God who sees light at the end of a long thin pipe and lets it in.

Let God divide them in half.

Let God share his Hoodsie.

Let the waters divide so that God may wash his face in first light.

Let there be pin holes in the sky in which God puts his little finger.

Let the stars be a heaven of jelly rolls and babies laughing.

Let the light be called Day so that men may grow corn or take busses.

Let there be on the second day dry land so that all men may dry their toes with Cannon towels.

Let God call this earth and feel the grasses rise up like angel hair.

Let there be bananas, cucumbers, prunes, mangoes, beans, rice and candy canes.

Let them seed and reseed.

Let there be seasons so that we may learn the architecture of the sky with eagles, finches, flickers, seagulls.

Let there be seasons so that we may put on twelve coats and shovel snow or take off our skins and bathe in the Carribean.

Let there be seasons so the sky dogs will jump across the sun in December.

Let there be seasons so that the eel may come out of her green cave.

Let there be seasons so that the raccoon may raise his blood level.

Let there be seasons so that the wind may be hoisted for an orange leaf.

Let there be seasons so that the rain will bury many ships.

Let there be seasons so that the miracles will fill our drinking glass with runny gold.

Let there be seasons so that our tongues will be rich in asparagus and limes.

Let there be seasons so that our fires will not forsake us and turn to metal.

Let there be seasons so that a man may close his palm on a woman's breast and bring forth a sweet nipple, a starberry.

Let there be a heaven so that man may outlive his grasses.

For I am an orphan with two death masks on the mantel and came from the grave of my mama's belly into the commerce of Boston.

For there were only two windows on the city and the buildings ate me.

For I was swaddled in grease wool from my father's company and could not move or ask the time.

For Anne and Christopher were born in my head as I howled at the grave of the roses, the ninety-four rose crèches of my bedroom.

For Christopher, my imaginary brother, my twin holding his baby cock like a minnow.

For I became a *we* and this imaginary *we* became a kind company when the big balloons did not bend over us.

For I could not read or speak and on the long nights I could not turn the moon off or count the lights of cars across the ceiling.

For I lay as pale as flour and drank moon juice from a rubber tip.

For I wet my pants and Christopher told the clock and it ticked like a July cricket and silently moved its spoons.

For I shat and Christopher smiled and said let the air be sweet with your soil.

For I listened to Christopher unless the balloon came and changed my bandage.

For my crotch itched and hands oiled it.

For I lay as single as death. Christopher lay beside me. He was living.

For I lay as stiff as the paper roses and Christopher took a tin basin and bathed me.

For I spoke not but the magician played me tricks of the blood.

For I heard not but for the magician lying beside me playing like a radio.

For I cried then and my little box wiggled with melancholy.

For I was in a boundary of wool and painted boards. Where are we Christopher? Jail, he said.

For the room itself was a box. Four thick walls of roses. A ceiling Christopher found low and menacing.

For I smiled and there was no one to notice. Christopher was asleep. He was making a sea sound.

For I wiggled my fingers but they would not stay. I could not put them in place. They broke out of my mouth.

For I was prodding myself out of my sleep, out the green room. The sleep of the desperate who travel backwards into darkness.

For birth was a disease and Christopher and I invented the cure.

For we swallow magic and we deliver Anne.

EIGHTH PSALM

No. No. The woman is cheerful, she smiles at her stomach. She has swallowed a bagful of oranges and she is well pleased.

For she has come through the voyage fit and her room carries the little people.

For she has outlived the dates in the back of Fords, she has outlived the penises of her teens to come here, to the married harbor.

For she is the forbidden one, telling time by her ten long fingers.

For she is the dangerous hills and many a climber will be lost on such a passage.

For she is lost from mankind; she is knitting her own hair into a baby shawl.

For she is stuffed by Christopher into a neat package that will not undo until the weeks pass.

For she is a magnitude, she is many. She is each of us patting ourselves dry with a towel.

For she is nourished by darkness.

For she is in the dark room putting bones into place.

For she is clustering the gold and the silver, the minerals and chemicals.

For she is a hoarder, she puts away silks and wools and lips and small white eyes.

For she is seeing the end of her confinement now and is waiting like a stone for the waters.

For the baby crowns and there is a people-dawn in the world.

For the baby lies in its water and blood and there is a people-cry in the world.

For the baby suckles and there is a people made of milk for her to use. There are milk trees to hiss her on. There are milk beds in which to lie and dream of a warm room. There are milk fingers to fold and unfold. There are milk bottoms that are wet and caressed and put into their cotton.

For there are many worlds of milk to walk through under the moon.

For the baby grows and the mother places her giggle-jog on her knee and sings a song of Christopher and Anne.

For the mother sings songs of the baby that knew.

For the mother remembers the baby she was and never locks and twists or puts lonely into a foreign place.

For the baby lives. The mother will die and when she does Christopher will go with her. Christopher who stabbed his kisses and cried up to make two out of one.

TENTH PSALM

For as the baby springs out like a starfish into her million light years Anne sees that she must climb her own mountain.

For as she eats wisdom like the halves of a pear she puts one foot in front of the other. She climbs the dark wing.

For as her child grows Anne grows and there is salt and cantaloupe and molasses for all.

For as Anne walks, the music walks and the family lies down in milk.

For I am not locked up.

For I am placing fist over fist on rock and plunging into the altitude of words. The silence of words.

For the husband sells his rain to God and God is well pleased with His family.

For they fling together against hardness and somewhere, in another room, a light is clicked on by gentle fingers.

For death comes to friends, to parents, to sisters. Death comes with its bagful of pain yet they do not curse the key they were given to hold.

For they open each door and it gives them a new day at the yellow window.

For the child grows to a woman, her breasts coming up like the moon while Anne rubs the peace stone.

For the child starts up her own mountain (not being locked in) and reaches the coastline of grapes.

For Anne and her daughter master the mountain and again and again. Then the child finds a man who opens like the sea.

For that daughter must build her own city and fill it with her own oranges, her own words.

For Anne walked up and up and finally over the years until she was old as the moon and with its naggy voice.

For Anne had climbed over eight mountains and saw the children washing the tiny statues in the square.

For Anne sat down with the blood of a hammer and built a tombstone for herself and Christopher sat beside her and was well pleased with their red shadow.

For they hung up a picture of a rat and the rat smiled and held out his hand.

For the rat was blessed on that mountain. He was given a white bath.

For the milk in the skies sank down upon them and tucked them in.

For God did not forsake them but put the blood angel to look after them until such time as they would enter their star.

For the sky dogs jumped out and shoveled snow upon us and we lay in our quiet blood.

For God was as large as a sunlamp and laughed his heat at us and therefore we did not cringe at the death hole.

Editors' Note:

In its original form in *The Death Notebooks*, the sequence "O Ye Tongues" consists of nine numbered psalms. *The Complete Poems* includes an addition to the sequence designated "Second Psalm" that changes all subsequent title numbers. This selection follows the titling in *The Complete Poems*.

From The Awful Rowing Toward God

(1975)

Rowing

A story, a story!
(Let it go. Let it come.)
I was stamped out like a Plymouth fender
into this world.
First came the crib
with its glacial bars.
Then dolls
and the devotion to their plastic mouths.
Then there was school,
the little straight rows of chairs,
blotting my name over and over,
but undersea all the time,
a stranger whose elbows wouldn't work.
Then there was life
with its cruel houses
and people who seldom touched —
though touch is all —
but I grew,
like a pig in a trenchcoat I grew,
and then there were many strange apparitions,
the nagging rain, the sun turning into poison
and all of that, saws working through my heart,
but I grew, I grew,
and God was there like an island I had not rowed to,
still ignorant of Him, my arms and my legs worked,
and I grew, I grew,
I wore rubies and bought tomatoes
and now, in my middle age,
about nineteen in the head I'd say,
I am rowing, I am rowing
though the oarlocks stick and are rusty
and the sea blinks and rolls
like a worried eyeball,

but I am rowing, I am rowing,
though the wind pushes me back
and I know that that island will not be perfect,
it will have the flaws of life,
the absurdities of the dinner table,
but there will be a door
and I will open it
and I will get rid of the rat inside of me,
the gnawing pestilential rat.
God will take it with his two hands
and embrace it.

As the African says:
This is my tale which I have told,
if it be sweet, if it be not sweet,
take somewhere else and let some return to me.
This story ends with me still rowing.

Riding the Elevator into the Sky

As the fireman said:
Don't book a room over the fifth floor
in any hotel in New York.
They have ladders that will reach further
but no one will climb them.
As the New York *Times* said:
The elevator always seeks out
the floor of the fire
and automatically opens
and won't shut.
These are the warnings
that you must forget
if you're climbing out of yourself.
If you're going to smash into the sky.

Many times I've gone past
the fifth floor,
cranking upward,
but only once
have I gone all the way up.
Sixtieth floor:
small plants and swans bending
into their grave.
Floor two hundred:
mountains with the patience of a cat,
silence wearing its sneakers.
Floor five hundred:
messages and letters centuries old,
birds to drink,
a kitchen of clouds.
Floor six thousand:
the stars,
skeletons on fire,

their arms singing.
And a key,
a very large key,
that opens something —
some useful door —
somewhere —
up there.

When Man Enters Woman

When man
enters woman,
like the surf biting the shore,
again and again,
and the woman opens her mouth in pleasure
and her teeth gleam
like the alphabet,
Logos appears milking a star,
and the man
inside of woman
ties a knot
so that they will
never again be separate
and the woman
climbs into a flower
and swallows its stem
and Logos appears
and unleashes their rivers.

This man,
this woman
with their double hunger,
have tried to reach through
the curtain of God
and briefly they have,
though God
in His perversity
unties the knot.

The Earth

God loafs around heaven,
without a shape
but He would like to smoke His cigar
or bite His fingernails
and so forth.

God owns heaven
but He craves the earth,
the earth with its little sleepy caves,
its bird resting at the kitchen window,
even its murders lined up like broken chairs,
even its writers digging into their souls
with jackhammers,
even its hucksters selling their animals
for gold,
even its babies sniffing for their music,
the farm house, white as a bone,
sitting in the lap of its corn,
even the statue holding up its widowed life,
even the ocean with its cupful of students,
but most of all He envies the bodies,
He who has no body.

The eyes, opening and shutting like keyholes
and never forgetting, recording by thousands,
the skull with its brains like eels —
the tablet of the world —
the bones and their joints
that build and break for any trick,
the genitals,
the ballast of the eternal,
and the heart, of course,
that swallows the tides
and spits them out cleansed.

He does not envy the soul so much.
He is all soul
but He would like to house it in a body
and come down
and give it a bath
now and then.

Jesus, the Actor, Plays the Holy Ghost

Oh, Mother,
Virgin Mother,
before the gulls take me out the door,
marry me.
Marry me not to a goat
but to a goddess.
What?
You say it can not be done!

Then I will do it!
I wash the crows
but they do not whiten.
I push out the desk,
pulling it from its roots.
I shave the caterpillar
but he is only a worm.
I take the yellow papers
and I write on them
but they crumble like men's ashes.
I take the daisy
and blow my heart into it
but it will not speak.

Oh, mother,
marry me,
before the gulls take me out the door.
Will I marry the dark earth,
the thief of the daylight?
Will I marry a tree
and only wave my hands at you
from your front yard?
Oh, mother,
oh, mother,
you marry me,
save me from the cockroach,

weave me into the sun.
There will be bread.
There will be water.
My elbows will be salt.

Oh, Mary,
Gentle Mother,
open the door and let me in.
A bee has stung your belly with faith.
Let me float in it like a fish.
Let me in! Let me in!
I have been born many times, a false Messiah,
but let me be born again
into something true.

Frenzy

I am not lazy.
I am on the amphetamine of the soul.
I am, each day,
typing out the God
my typewriter believes in.
Very quick. Very intense,
like a wolf at a live heart.
Not lazy.
When a lazy man, they say,
looks toward heaven,
the angels close the windows.

Oh angels,
keep the windows open
so that I may reach in
and steal each object,
objects that tell me the sea is not dying,
objects that tell me the dirt has a life-wish,
that the Christ who walked for me,
walked on true ground
and that this frenzy,
like bees stinging the heart all morning,
will keep the angels
with their windows open,
wide as an English bathtub.

The God-Monger

With all my questions,
all the nihilistic words in my head,
I went in search of an answer,
I went in search of the other world
which I reached by digging underground,
past the stones as solemn as preachers,
past the roots, throbbing like veins
and went in search of some animal of wisdom,
and went in search, it could be said,
of my husband (i.e. the one who carries you through).

Down.
Down.
Down.
There I found a mouse
with trees growing out of his belly.
He was all wise.
He was my husband.
Yet he was silent.

He did three things.
He extruded a gourd of water.
Then I hit him on the head,
gently, a hit more like a knock.
Then he extruded a gourd of beer.
I knocked once more
and finally a dish of gravy.

Those were my answers.
Water. Beer. Food.
I was not satisfied.

Though the mouse
had not licked my leprous skin
that was my final answer.

The soul was not cured,
it was as full as a clothes closet
of dresses that did not fit.
Water. Beer. Gravy.
It simply had to be enough.
Husband,
who am I to reject the naming of foods
in a time of famine?

Small Wire

My faith
is a great weight
hung on a small wire,
as doth the spider
hang her baby on a thin web,
as doth the vine,
twiggy and wooden,
hold up grapes
like eyeballs,
as many angels
dance on the head of a pin.

God does not need
too much wire to keep Him there,
just a thin vein,
with blood pushing back and forth in it,
and some love.
As it has been said:
Love and a cough
cannot be concealed.
Even a small cough.
Even a small love.
So if you have only a thin wire,
God does not mind.
He will enter your hands
as easily as ten cents used to
bring forth a Coke.

The Rowing Endeth

I'm mooring my rowboat
at the dock of the island called God.
This dock is made in the shape of a fish
and there are many boats moored
at many different docks.
"It's okay," I say to myself,
with blisters that broke and healed
and broke and healed —
saving themselves over and over.
And salt sticking to my face and arms like
a glue-skin pocked with grains of tapioca.
I empty myself from my wooden boat
and onto the flesh of The Island.

"On with it!" He says and thus
we squat on the rocks by the sea
and play ——— can it be true ———
a game of poker.
He calls me.
I win because I hold a royal straight flush.
He wins because He holds five aces.
A wild card had been announced
but I had not heard it
being in such a state of awe
when He took out the cards and dealt.
As he plunks down His five aces
and I sit grinning at my royal flush,
He starts to laugh,
the laughter rolling like a hoop out of His mouth
and into mine,
and such laughter that He doubles right over me
laughing a Rejoice-Chorus at our two triumphs.
Then I laugh, the fishy dock laughs
the sea laughs. The Island laughs.
The Absurd laughs.

Dearest dealer,
I with my royal straight flush,
love you so for your wild card,
that untamable, eternal, gut-driven *ha-ha*
and lucky love.

Posthumously Published Work

45 Mercy Street

From **Beginning the Hegira**

The Money Swing

After "Babylon Revisited" by F. Scott Fitzgerald

Mother, Father,
I hold this snapshot of you,
taken, it says, in 1929
on the deck of the yawl.
Mother, Father,
so young, so hot, so jazzy,
so like Zelda and Scott
with drinks and cigarettes and turbans
and designer slacks and frizzy permanents
and all that dough,
what do you say to me now,
here at my sweaty desk in 1971?

I know the ice in your drink is senile.
I know your smile will develop a boil.
You know only that you are on top,
swinging like children on the money swing
up and over, up and over,
until even New York City lies down small.
You know that when winter comes
and the snow comes
that it won't be real snow.
If you don't want it to be snow
you just pay money.

Food

I want mother's milk,
that good sour soup.
I want breasts singing like eggplants,
and a mouth above making kisses.
I want nipples like shy strawberries
for I need to suck the sky.
I need to bite also
as in a carrot stick.
I need arms that rock,
two clean clam shells singing *ocean*.
Further I need weeds to eat
for they are the spinach of the soul.
I am hungry and you give me
a dictionary to decipher.
I am a baby all wrapped up in its red howl
and you pour salt into my mouth.
Your nipples are stitched up like sutures
and although I suck
I suck air
and even the big fat sugar moves away.
Tell me! Tell me! Why is it?
I need food
and you walk away reading the paper.

From **Bestiary U.S.A.**

Hornet

A red-hot needle
hangs out of him, he steers by it
as if it were a rudder, he
would get in the house any way he could
and then he would bounce from window
to ceiling, buzzing and looking for you.
Do not sleep for he is there wrapped in the curtain.
Do not sleep for he is there under the shelf.
Do not sleep for he wants to sew up your skin,
he wants to leap into your body like a hammer
with a nail, do not sleep he wants to get into
your nose and make a transplant, he wants do not
sleep he wants to bury your fur and make
a nest of knives, he wants to slide under your
fingernail and push in a splinter, do not sleep
he wants to climb out of the toilet when you sit on it
and make a home in the embarrassed hair do not sleep
he wants you to walk into him as into a dark fire.

Star-Nosed Mole

Mole, angel-dog of the pit,
digging six miles a night,
what's up with you in your sooty suit,
where's your kitchen at?

I find you at the edge of our pond,
drowned, numb drainer of weeds,
insects floating in your belly,
grubs like little fetuses bobbing

and your dear face with its fifth hand,
doesn't it know it's the end of the war?
It's all over, no need to go deep into ponds,
no fires, no cripples left.

               Mole dog,
I wish your mother would wake you up
and you wouldn't lie there like the Pietà
wearing your cross on your nose.

Whale

Whale on the beach, you dinosaur,
what brought you smoothing into this dead harbor?
If you'd stayed inside you could have grown
as big as the Empire State. Still you are not a fish,
perhaps you like the land, you'd had enough of
holding your breath under water. What is it we want
of you? To take our warm blood into the great sea
and prove we are not the sufferers of God?
We are sick of babies crying and the birds flapping
loose in the air. We want the double to be big,
and ominous and we want to remember when you were
money in Massachusetts and yet were wild and rude
and killers. We want our killers dressed in black
like grease for we are sick of writing checks,
putting on our socks and working in the little boxes
we call the office.

Where It Was At Back Then

Husband,
last night I dreamt
they cut off your hands and feet.
Husband,
you whispered to me,
Now we are both incomplete.

Husband,
I held all four
in my arms like sons and daughters.
Husband,
I bent slowly down
and washed them in magical waters.

Husband,
I placed each one
where it belonged on you.
"A miracle,"
you said and we laughed
the laugh of the well-to-do.

Divorce, Thy Name Is Woman

I am divorcing daddy — Dybbuk! Dybbuk!
I have been doing it daily all my life
since his sperm left him
drilling upwards and stuck to an egg.
Fetus, fetus — glows and glows in that home
and bursts out, electric, demanding moths.

For years it was woman to woman,
breast, crib, toilet, dolls, dress-ups.
WOMAN! WOMAN!
Daddy of the whiskies, daddy of the rooster breath,
would visit and then dash away
as if I were a disease.

Later,
when blood and eggs and breasts
dropped onto me,
Daddy and his whiskey breath
made a long midnight visit
in a dream that is not a dream
and then called his lawyer quickly.
Daddy divorcing me.

I have been divorcing him ever since,
going into court with Mother as my witness
and both long dead or not
I am still divorcing him,
adding up the crimes
of how he came to me,
how he left me.

I am pacing the bedroom.
Opening and shutting the windows.
Making the bed and pulling it apart.
I am tearing the feathers out of the pillows,
waiting, waiting for Daddy to come home
and stuff me so full of our infected child
that I turn invisible, but married,
at last.

The Consecrating Mother

I stand before the sea
and it rolls and rolls in its green blood
saying, "Do not give up one god
for I have a handful."
The trade winds blew
in their twelve-fingered reversal
and I simply stood on the beach
while the ocean made a cross of salt
and hung up its drowned
and they cried *Deo Deo*.
The ocean offered them up in the vein of its might.
I wanted to share this
but I stood alone like a pink scarecrow.
The ocean steamed in and out,
the ocean gasped upon the shore
but I could not define her,
I could not name her mood, her locked-up faces.
Far off she rolled and rolled
like a woman in labor
and I thought of those who had crossed her,
in antiquity, in nautical trade, in slavery, in war.
I wondered how she had borne those bulwarks.
She should be entered skin to skin,
and put on like one's first or last cloth,
entered like kneeling your way into church,
descending into that ascension,
though she be slick as olive oil,
as she climbs each wave like an embezzler of white.
The big deep knows the law as it wears its gray hat,
though the ocean comes in its destiny,
with its one hundred lips,
and in moonlight she comes in *her* nudity,
flashing breasts made of milk-water,

flashing buttocks made of unkillable lust,
and at night when you enter her
you shine like a neon soprano.

I am that clumsy human
on the shore
loving you, coming, coming,
going,
and wish to put my thumb on you
like The Song of Solomon.

Words for Dr. Y.

From **Letters to Dr. Y.**

[What has it come to, Dr. Y.]

What has it come to, Dr. Y.
my needing you?
I work days,
stuffed into a pine-paneled box.
You work days
with your air conditioner gasping
like a tube-fed woman.
I move my thin legs into your office
and we work over the cadaver of my soul.
We make a stage set out of my past
and stuff painted puppets into it.
We make a bridge toward my future
and I cry to you: I will be steel!
I will build a steel bridge over my need!
I will build a bomb shelter over my heart!
But my future is a secret.
It is as shy as a mole.

What has it come to
my needing you . . .
I am the irritating pearl
and you are the necessary shell.
You are the twelve faces of the Atlantic
and I am the rowboat. I am the burden.

How dependent, the fox asks?
Why so needy, the snake sings?
It's this way . . .
Time after time I fall down into the well
and you dig a tunnel in the dangerous sand,
you take the altar from a church and shore it up.

With your own white hands you dig me out.
You give me hoses so I can breathe.
You make me a skull to hold the worms
of my brains. You give me hot chocolate
although I am known to have no belly.
The trees are whores yet you place
me under them. The sun is poison
yet you toss me under it like a rose.
I am out of practice at living.
You are as brave as a motorcycle.

What has it come to
that I should defy you?
I would be a copper wire
without electricity.
I would be a Beacon Hill dowager
without her hat.
I would be a surgeon
who cut with his own nails.
I would be a glutton
who threw away his spoon.
I would be God
without Jesus to speak for me.

I would be Jesus
without a cross to prove me.

[I called him *Comfort*]

I called him *Comfort*.
Dr. Y., I gave him the wrong name.
I should have called him *Preacher*
for all day there on the coastland
he read me the Bible.
He read me the Bible to prove I was sinful.
For in the night he was betrayed.
And then he let me give him a Judas-kiss,
that red lock that held us in place,
and then I gave him a drink from my cup
and he whispered, "Rape, rape."
And then I gave him my wrist
and he sucked on the blood,
hating himself for it,
murmuring, "God will see. God will see."

And I said,
"To hell with God!"

And he said,
"Would you mock God?"

And I said,
"God is only mocked by believers!"

And he said,
"I love only the truth."

And I said,
"This holy concern for the truth —
no one worries about it except liars."

And God was bored.
He turned on his side
like an opium eater
and slept.

[It's music you've never heard]

It's music you've never heard
that I've heard,
that makes me think of you —
not Villa Lobos, my heart's media,
but pop songs on my kitchen radio
bleating like a goat.
I know a little bit
about a lot of things
but I don't know enough about you . . .
Songs like cherries in a bowl,
sweet and sour and small.
Suddenly I'm not half the girl
I used to be.
There's a shadow hanging over me . . .
From me to you out of my electric devil
but easy like the long skirts
in a Renoir picnic with clouds and parasols.

Fourteen boys in cars are parked
with fourteen girls in cars and they
are listening to our song with one blood.
No one is ruined. Everyone is in
a delight at this ardor.

I am in a delight with you, Music Man.
Your name is Dr. Y. My name is Anne.

[I'm dreaming the My Lai soldier again]

I'm dreaming the My Lai soldier again,
I'm dreaming the My Lai soldier night after night.
He rings the doorbell like the Fuller Brush Man
and wants to shake hands with me
and I do because it would be rude to say no
and I look at my hand and it is green
with intestines.
And they won't come off,
they won't. He apologizes for this over and over.
The My Lai soldier lifts me up again and again
and lowers me down with the other dead women and babies
saying, *It's my job. It's my job.*

Then he gives me a bullet to swallow
like a sleeping tablet.
I am lying in this belly of dead babies
each one belching up the yellow gasses of death
and their mothers tumble, eyeballs, knees, upon me,
each for the last time, each authentically dead.
The soldier stands on a stepladder above us
pointing his red penis right at me and saying,
Don't take this personally.

January 24th

Originality is important.

I am alone here in my own mind.
There is no map
and there is no road.
It is one of a kind
just as yours is.
It's in a vapor. It's in a flap.
It makes jelly. It chews toads.
It's a dummy. It's a whiz.
Sometimes I have to hunt her down.
Sometimes I have to track her.
Sometimes I hold her still and use a nutcracker.
Such conceit! Such maggoty thoughts,
such an enormous con
just cracks me up.
My brown study will do me in
gushing out of me cold or hot.
Yet I'd risk my life
on that dilly dally buttercup
called dreams. She of the origin,
she of the primal crack, she of the boiling
beginning, she of the riddle, she keeps me here,
toiling and toiling.

February 3rd

Your own ideas may be too fanciful to be practical.

My ideas are a curse.
They spring from a radical discontent
with the awful order of things.
I play clown. I play carpenter. I play nurse.
I play witch. Each like an advertisement
for change. My husband always plays King
and is continually shopping in his head for a queen
when only clown, carpenter, nurse, witch can be seen.

Take my LIBRARY CAPER.
I took thirty experts from our town
and each bought thirty expert books.
On an October night when witchery can occur
we each stole thirty books, we took them down
from the town library shelves, each of us a crook,
and placed them in the town dump, all that lovely paper.
We left our expert books upon the shelves. My library caper.

One night we crashed a wedding dinner,
but not the guests. We crashed the chef.
We put dollar bills in the salad, right beside
the lettuce and tomatoes. Our salad was a winner.
The guests kept picking out the bucks, such tiny thefts,
and cawing and laughing like seagulls at their landslide.
There was a strange power to it. Power in that lovely paper.
The bride and groom were proud. I call it my Buck Wedding
    Caper.

My own ideas are a curse for a king and a queen.
I'm a wound without blood, a car without gasoline
unless I can shake myself free of my dog, my flag,
of my desk, my mind, I find life a bit of a drag.
Not always, mind you. Usually I'm like my frying pan —
useful, graceful, sturdy and with no caper, no plan.

263

February 21st

The day is favorable for teamwork.

The photograph where we smile
at each other, dark head to light head,
sits on my desk. It lay unkissed all week.
That photograph walked up the aisle
for the twenty-three years we've been wed
on onward into Carolina, cheek to cheek.
Husband, mad hammer, man of force.
This last week has been our divorce.

I'm not a war baby. I'm a baby
at war. Thumbs grow into my throat.
I wear slaps like a spot of rouge.
Woodsman, who made me into your tree?
Drowner, who made me into your boat?
Lover, I feel a darkness, I feel a fugue
come over us. The photo sits over my desk
as we dance the karate, the mad burlesque.

From Last Poems

In Excelsis

It is half winter, half spring,
and Barbara and I are standing
confronting the ocean.
Its mouth is open very wide,
and it has dug up its green,
throwing it, throwing it at the shore.
You say it is angry.
I say it is like a kicked Madonna.
Its womb collapses, drunk with its fever.
We breathe in its fury.

I, the inlander,
am here with you for just a small space.
I am almost afraid,
so long gone from the sea.
I have seen her smooth as a cheek.
I have seen her easy,
doing her business,
lapping in.
I have seen her rolling her hoops of blue.
I have seen her tear the land off.
I have seen her drown me twice,
and yet not take me.
You tell me that as the green drains backward
it covers Britain,
but have you never stood on *that* shore
and seen it cover you?

We have come to worship,
the tongues of the surf are prayers,
and we vow,
the unspeakable vow.
Both silently.
Both differently.
I wish to enter her like a dream,
leaving my roots here on the beach
like a pan of knives.
And my past to unravel, with its knots and snarls,
and walk into ocean,
letting it explode over me
and outward, where I would drink the moon
and my clothes would slip away,
and I would sink into the great mother arms
I never had,
except here where the abyss
throws itself on the sand
blow by blow,
over and over,
and we stand on the shore
loving its pulse
as it swallows the stars,
and has since it all began
and will continue into oblivion,
past our knowing
and the wild toppling green that enters us today,
for a small time
in half winter, half spring.